Home Bistro

Also by Betty Fussell

Home Bistro

Simple, Sensual Fare in the Comfort of Your Own Kitchen

Betty Fussell

Wine Selections by David Rosengarten
and Joshua Wesson

THE ECCO PRESS

THE ECCO PRESS
100 West Broad Street
Hopewell, New Jersey 08525

Published simultaneously in Canada by
Penguin Books Canada Ltd., Ontario
Printed in the United States of America

Home Bistro is a revised and expanded compilation of *Eating In* (first published in 1986) and *Betty Fussell's Home Plates* (first published in 1990).

Library of Congress Cataloging-in-Publication Data
Fussell, Betty Harper.
    Home bistro : simple, sensual fare in the comfort of your kitchen / by Betty
Fussell
        p.   cm.
    Includes index.
    ISBN 0-88001-526-8
    1. Cookery, American. 2. Entertaining. I. Title.
    TX715.F97797   1997
    641.5973—dc20   96-43197

Designed by Barbara Cohen Aronica
The text of this book is set in Caslon

9 8 7 6 5 4 3 2 1

FIRST EDITION

Contents

For the most part, the recipes in this book are designed as one-dish meals for two people. Recipe ingredients may be doubled or tripled to serve four or six as needed

Introduction

I've said it before and I'll say it again. Thank God for eating out. It makes eating *in* such a pleasure. After a long day's work, do I dream of a long night's wait elbow-to-belly in a packed restaurant bar, eardrums shattered by the din of compulsory conviviality, wallet depleted, and tongue shriveled by the touted house wine? No, fellow worker, dreamer, eater, compadre. I dream of a tiny island of quiet where I call the shots, arrange the pleasures, create the events, and afterward fall into bed instead of a taxi. In this dream kingdom the simplest bowl of pasta, with say a little lemon and cream and maybe some asparagus, reeks of *eros* and *agape* because from creation to consummation I am the master of its fate. This fosters the illusion that I'm the master of my own. And I'll drink to that, with a bottle of sparkling Reisling at a third of the price demanded by my local bistro.

My local bistro? Which one? In the last decade bistros have multiplied like termites in a woodpile. But don't get me wrong. Bistros are my kind of place. Not because they began in France a century ago as wine taverns. Nor because the word may have come from a Russian word for "quickly" or a French word for "rotgut." Actually, no one knows where the word came from, but we do know what the word conveys now—a place to get a drink and a bite to eat in our working clothes, with elbows on the bar and a bowl of soup to sop our bread in. Unless you live in a mansion with a butler and footmen, a bistro spells home.

Home for me is a place you can cook in. But I have many friends, including my grown children, who don't take the same pleasure in cooking that I do. Eating, of course, is another matter. Some of the people I love best are people who love good food on the plate and good wine in the glass, who have excellent palates from eating out or living in with crafty cooks, but who'd never dream of spending an hour, a half hour, ten minutes even, at a stove.

A decade ago I wanted to convince these friends, and particularly men whose women had either died, divorced, or gone to work outside the kitchen, how easy it is to create something tasty by throwing together a few good ingredients. It's not technique but ingredients that count. At least when you cook and eat at home. So I threw some recipes together under the title *Eating In* and then some more under the title *Home Plates,* as more and more friends, again including my children, began to see that cooking was not only about good food on the plate but about the fun of getting it there. About the fun of exploring, adventuring, improvising, of creating something that wasn't there before, of juggling flavors and textures, of designing something to suit yourself. In custom-made cooking, you call all the shots.

So now I've put the two books together into one and stirred in a new batch of recipes for dishes I like to make at home, whether I'm cooking for my most constant and greedy companion—myself—or for a pal. I like cooking for myself best because I am never alone. Each ingredient speaks out, separately and together, and sometimes the noise is deafening. The onions may hiss, the garlic snap, the shrimp giggle and blush. With such relentless converse, who needs the distraction of human talk?

This is how it is for me now, but once upon a time it was different. I demanded an audience and applause, for I made my kitchen into a theater to show off in. I thought nothing of slaving twelve hours a day seven days a week to produce an *opera bouffe* of ballotines and galantines, mousses and soufflés, hollandaises and mayonnaises, pâtés and pâté-a-chouxs, all to display the magical transformation of housewife and home cook into masterful French chef. Those who lived through the sixties and the 1,239 pages of volumes one and two of Julia Child will know whereof I speak and will recognize in me an authentic period piece.

But now it's not opera I want, my own or other people's, and particularly not French opera. The more the world goes global, the more I discover the distinctly American pleasure of welcoming all comers to my skillet or wok. I've tossed out imperial French "rules" of exclusivity and now cross cultural borders with impunity. For the price of a subway token in my big city, I can command the globe in a babble of culinary languages. I don't have to spend money on travel. The world has come to me. Within the confines of a single store (albeit a very good one) and within the confines of a single sound (let's pick "ch" as in "cha-cha"), I can buy chayote, chanterelle, chapatti, cheesecake, chorizo, chickpeas, chèvre, challah, cherrystones, cherimoya, Chinese cabbage, chinook salmon, chuck roast, chutney—but why go on? As a cook the world is my oyster and the opener is in my hand.

But as I say, I've grown humble. Forget the cook and look to the ingredients. The buttery flesh of salmon, the smell of lemongrass, the velvet of coconut cream. This stunningly rich and diverse sensual world is always there to feed body and mind, waiting to be discovered for the very first time—in your or my kitchen, plate, palate. Cooking has always been a personal voyage of discovery and now that food can fly, each home can be a global bistro and our palates are the better for it.

Think of these recipes, then, as a stationary traveler's jottings, notes for improvisations, ideas to trigger your own. Wherever you are, buy what looks good in the market, what looks freshest, ripest, best. Look fish in the eye. Smell the bottom of a melon. Press an avocado gently in your palm. Pray over the peaches. As the ingredient goes, so goes the meal. I've made a dinner of fresh crisp green beans, sprinkled with a handful of walnuts toasted in golden olive oil. Simplest is best but the quality must be there. Quality is spelled F-R-E-S-H, whether it's cornmeal freshly ground or cherries freshly picked.

But of course you need staples in your kitchen that are not fresh but processed for shelf life: sugar and flour, olive oil, balsamic and wine vinegars, sea salt and soy sauce, dried chilies and beans and rice. I also keep anchovies and olives, sardines and canned tomatoes, dried pastas and mushrooms, and always lots of dried fruits. You also need staples that are somewhat more fragile, and thank God for refrigerators in which to keep butter, eggs, and cheese, fresh herbs like parsley and cilantro, fresh seasoners like lemons and limes. The point is to always have something on hand.

I have a contrary friend whose cupboard is always bare. So is her fridge, except for diet drinks and a half-emptied bottle of wine and a few rolls of film. "Why don't you lay in supplies so you'll always have something to work with?" I ask her. "Because I never know what I want to eat until I see it ready made in the store," she answers. I wish this book were for her, but it's not. She will never translate the ingredients on a page into a pot in her head and imagine how delicious the result. She will never salivate from a cookbook. She's a literalist. Put the dish in her face and her appetite quickens, but at no other time does food flit through her mind.

This book is for people who do salivate just by reading the words Orange-Cranberry Soup, Sweet Corn and Caviar, Pasta with Avocado Cream, Wood-Smoked Salmon in Orange Butter, Polenta Foie Gras. The words convey familiar and treasured friends in new couplings, to produce—as couplings always do—something different from their individual selves. Something we taste in our minds and instantly want to taste in our mouths. This book is for people with a strong mind-body connection, for sensualists of the imagination who can put their fantasies into action in the privacy and security of their home bistro.

Remember that these recipes are designed in large part as one-dish meals for two people. It's more efficient to shop and cook for two than for one, and if you're lucky enough to be alone you've got a built-in doggie bag for the morrow. You can always double the quantities in a recipe for four, triple them for six, quadruple them for eight. But if you're cooking regularly for eight, you'd better stick to the Pasta and Polenta section, and insist on eating out at least twice a week.

Just as we've radicalized our notions of what ingredients go together, so we've radicalized our notions of what constitutes a meal. We've abandoned what seemed to be the eternal British triangle of meat-potatoes-vegetables in favor of a single dish of pasta, rice, soup, stew, a platter of roasted vegetables, a large salad, a bowl of fruit. We've even thrown out the menu triangle of soup-main dish-dessert, with soup at the apex and dessert at the ever-widening bottom.

More and more we want intensity and variety rather than quantity. More and more we like the idea of browsing through several small plates, as in Chinese *dim sum*, Middle Eastern *mezes*, Spanish *tapas*. In our home bistro we can create this variety over the course of a week instead of at a single meal and at the same time we can loosen up that orthodox dietetic concept of "balance."

A single dish at a single meal is not only thrifty of time and labor, it allows you to concentrate on the distinctive pleasures of the ingredients of that one dish. Like an ex-president not known for his fine palate, I'm not mad for broccoli, but I won't easily forget how delicious a head of broccoli was when I made a meal of it, carefully peeling the stems so that they would cook quickly with the flowerets when I sautéed them in sweet butter, seasoned only with salt and pepper and a dribble of sesame oil. What could be simpler? But every bite was the essence of green, crisp and tender. It was like eating a garden, and because I ate the whole head, my body said, yes, thanks, I'm full.

Was this a balanced meal? Of course not. But am I going to eat nothing but broccoli day in and day out? Of course not. We who have the luxury of choice need not be neurotic about balancing each meal or even each week or each month. Provided that we're not regularly overloading a single circuit such as sugar or fat, whether the circuit is overt or concealed, and provided that we act on what we know and don't cheat on ourselves. Our bodies are full of common sense if we haven't corrupted them with our fears and lies and psychoses. All we have to do is let the body speak, the way ingredients do, if only we have ears to hear.

This said, we often want diversity within a single meal, so I've noted for the majority of recipes other foods that make good companions. We all need ideas from time to time, and it's good to feed on other people's. That's what recipes are for. More importantly, we've got our wine experts David Rosengarten and Josh Wesson to contribute wine suggestions because that's what wine experts are for. And now that the world of wines has exploded as globally as foods, most of us need all the help we can get because so much of the time our shops will have wines we never heard of from countries we never knew existed. Again, an open mind is the best kind to have and experimentation in mixing and matching tastes to find your own favorites is the best way to go.

For tastes are not only individual. They change. I find that I respond madly now to sweet dessert wines, have a real hunger for them, and that spills over into a renewed appreciation for white wines such as Rieslings and Gewürztraminers and other Alsatian/Germanic wines that have been out of favor in the prolonged "dry" period of whites. I think my stomach has rusted out from too much dry and is telling me to sweeten it up a bit.

Simple food, simple methods. My *batterie de cuisine* gets simpler every year. Despite a woodblock full of culinarily correct and well-sharpened chef knives, I find myself using for everything a $3.95 dishwasher-proof four-inch knife with serrated edge that I found in a hardware store in the old Italian market of Philadelphia. I'm sure this cheapo knife is for sale in many places, but I now buy it in quantity from this store to give away to friends.

In the same way, I find I use my wok for everything. Contrary to the recent advice of a cooking magazine that said throw out your wok because it was built for a brasier, I would no more throw out my wok than my blender. And this isn't a fancy wok on a stand to keep its round bottom from tipping. This is your ordinary cheapo wok from Chinatown, but well seasoned and useful for everything from smoking to steaming to deep frying. With my knife and wok I could cook up a little something anywhere in the world, including the Sahara. But I would prefer to take along my blender and, as long as electricity is called for, a food processor. But that's because I'm lazy, not because I gotta have it. A blender is a necessity, a food processor a luxury, and I use both all the time.

Because doing my own thing in the kitchen has turned out to be one of my most lasting pleasures and certainly my most daily one, I can't help but encourage others to join in the fun. I like being in control of my stove, my stomach, my table, my home place. There's so much I'm not in control of, in a city with exploding gas mains, ear-splitting sirens, stalled subways, hostile beggars, friendly muggers, supercilious waiters, skyscraper prices, and a heart-attack pulse. Like anyone with whom you've had a lifelong romance, sometimes you love it and sometimes you hate it. But the romance with food is an island romance, as steadfast as slippers or your favorite chair, as Mozart or Armstrong on the stereo, as framed photos on the wall or memories in the heart. This romance is consummated every day by the long, slow savoring of the harvests of sea and land, in the bistro I call home.

Home Bistro

Starters and Nibbles

Tapenade Dip
Salsas: Jícama-Tomatillo and Cranberry-Jalapeño
Fresh Potato Chips
Roast Potato Chips
Baked French Fries
Wild Mushroom Pâté
Fresh Corn and Caviar
Truffled Eggs
Yogurt Eggs
Sweet Corn and Onion Frittata
Crab and Avocado Omelet
Onion-Cheese Soufflé
Scallops Seviche
Roasted Oysters with Curry Butter
Chinese Shrimp-in-the-Shell
Wok-Smoked Trout
Smoked Haddock Brandade
Smoked Salmon and Mascarpone Terrine
Green Chili Soup
Chili-Carrot Soup
Red Pepper-Garlic Soup
Corn and Sorrel Soup
Daikon and Mint Soup
Orange-Cranberry Soup
White Bean and Burnt Almond Soup

Tapenade Dip

Raw vegetables (carrots, fennel, celery, cauliflower and broccoli flowerets, zucchini, snow peas, etc.)
½ cup black Mediterranean olives, pitted
1 clove garlic, mashed
1 tablespoon drained capers
4 anchovy fillets
1 egg yolk
1 teaspoon Dijon mustard
1 tablespoon fresh lemon juice
¼ cup olive oil
1 tablespoon chopped fresh basil or parsley, or other herbs

Prepare the vegetables and arrange on a platter.

Put the olives, garlic, capers, anchovies, egg, mustard, and lemon juice in a blender and purée until smooth. With the motor running, add the olive oil in a thin stream until it is absorbed by the purée. Put the sauce in a bowl, and garnish with the basil.

Instead of vegetables, use cooked shrimp, broiled sea scallops, or toasted French bread.

Jícama–Tomatillo Salsa

½ cup jícama, diced fine
½ cup tomatillos, husked and diced fine
1 jalapeño pepper, seeded and minced
2 tablespoons fresh cilantro, chopped
1 tablespoon fresh lime juice
2 tablespoons olive oil
Salt and black pepper

In a small bowl, mix all the ingredients, cover, and chill for an hour before serving with a basket of corn chips.

Cranberry–Jalapeño Salsa

½ cup cranberries
1 jalapeño pepper, seeded and minced
1 mandarin orange, peeled and chopped
1 tablespoon olive oil
1 tablespoon honey, or to taste
¼ teaspoon cinnamon

Chop the cranberries in a food processor and mix with the other ingredients. Cover and chill for an hour before serving with a basket of corn chips.

Fresh Potato Chips

4 cups vegetable oil or lard
2 Idaho baking potatoes
Salt and black and cayenne peppers

Heat 1 to 2 inches of oil in a wok or deep skillet.

Scrub the potatoes well but don't peel them. Cut them into thin slices (⅛-inch thick) in a food processor or by hand and pat them dry with paper towels.

When the oil is hot but not smoking (when a test slice of potato bubbles and floats on the top), add the potatoes a few slices at a time (to keep the oil hot) until they go limp. Remove with a slotted spoon and drain on paper towels. Let the slices rest for 10 minutes or more.

Reheat the oil and refry the slices until they are crisp and browned, 2 to 4 minutes. Drain again on paper towels and season to taste. Eat immediately.

Roasted Potato Chips

2 Idaho potatoes
Salt and black pepper
4 tablespoons olive oil

Scrub potatoes but leave skins on. Slice paper-thin with the slicing disk of a food processor or slice by hand.

Brush a baking sheet with olive oil. Lay the slices in a single layer on top of the oil, then turn them over (so they're oiled on both sides) and season with salt and pepper. Bake at 350°F. about 30 minutes, or until crisped and browned but not burned.

◆ Good by themselves to serve with drinks instead of store-bought potato chips.

◆ Make a fancy potato dish by layering oiled slices in a shallow baking pan, dotting them with a little butter and fresh herbs, such as thyme, and then sprinkling with fresh lemon juice and grated Parmesan cheese. Bake at 400°F. for about 45 to 50 minutes, until potatoes are tender.

Baked French Fries

2 large Idaho potatoes
2 tablespoons olive oil
1 teaspoon salt

Peel the potatoes, cut them lengthwise into ¼-inch slices, then cut each slice lengthwise into ¼-inch strips. Soak the strips in a bowl of ice water for 10 minutes. Drain and dry them thoroughly with paper towels.

Lay the slices in a single layer on an oiled baking sheet, then brush them with oil and sprinkle with salt. Bake at 375°F. for 40 minutes, then turn each strip to brown the other side for 10 to 15 minutes more.

◆ Dip them as the French and Californians do into a little bowl of mustard-mayonnaise.

Wild Mushroom Pâté

½ pound wild mushrooms (shiitake, oyster, morel, chanterelle)
4 tablespoons butter
1 green onion with top, chopped
2 tablespoons hazelnuts, skins on, chopped fine
½ teaspoon Worcestershire sauce
1 to 2 tablespoons brandy
Salt and black and cayenne peppers

Cut off the root end of the mushroom stems if they are sandy and discard. Slice mushrooms and their stems. Heat butter in a large skillet over high heat. Brown mushrooms and onion about 4 minutes. Add chopped nuts and brown 1 minute. Lower heat and cook for 2 more minutes to release mushroom juices. Put mixture in a food processor, add Worcestershire, brandy, and seasonings, and pulse until mixture is finely chopped. Pack pâté into a pottery bowl for serving (keeps well refrigerated for about a week).

◆ Serve on toast or in pita halves.

◆ Serve as a salad by piling mushroom mixture on a bed of arugula, watercress, or mixed garden greens. Or, surround the mushroom mixture with slices of smoked chicken or turkey breast, with sliced avocado, or spears of crisp asparagus.

Fresh Corn and Caviar

¼ cup good sturgeon (or whitefish or salmon) caviar
1 cup fresh corn kernels
2 tablespoons sweet onion, finely minced

Mix the ingredients together lightly in a glass bowl and chill for an hour. Serve on triangles of buttered white toast, crusts removed.

◆ This also makes a good filling for an omelet, adding a dollop of sour cream, or as a garnish for raw oysters or broiled fish.

Truffled Eggs

2 fresh black truffles
6 eggs
Salt and black pepper
6 tablespoons butter

Clean the truffles by scrubbing them with a vegetable brush under cold running water; then dice them fine.

In a medium bowl, beat the eggs with the salt and pepper, and stir in the truffles (if you have any time before eating, put the mixture in an airtight container to get maximum truffle symbiosis).

Melt the butter in a nonstick or well-seasoned skillet. Add the eggs and cook gently over very low heat, stirring constantly with a spatula or wooden spoon to cook the eggs evenly. While the eggs are still soft and almost runny, scoop them onto warm plates.

◆ Serve with toasted pita halves, English muffins, or croissants. Follow with a green salad, ripe pears, and chèvre.

◆ Make a Truffled Omelet. For each person, use ½ truffle and 2 tablespoons diced foie gras pâté to 3 eggs. Cook one omelet at a time. Mix the diced truffles and pâté together. Heat 1½ tablespoons of butter until it is bubbling, and add the beaten eggs. With the back of a fork, push the edges of the cooked eggs toward the middle of the pan. Top each omelet with half the truffle mixture. Fold the omelet over as you slide it onto a plate. For detailed instructions, see Crab and Avocado Omelet.

◆ Try a sparkling rosé to play off the earthiness of the truffles: Bouvet is a good choice from the Loire or, for a special treat, look for Charbaut.

Yogurt Eggs

2 tablespoons each *olive oil and butter*
4 large eggs
Salt and black pepper
1 cup plain yogurt
2 green onions with tops, chopped, for garnish

Heat oil and butter in a large skillet over low heat. Beat eggs with seasonings and add to skillet, stirring slowly in one direction. When they are just set, remove from heat and stir in yogurt. Sprinkle top with green onions.

◆ Serve with toasted pita halves or bagel chips.

◆ Yogurt is also good as a topping for fried eggs, hard- or soft-cooked eggs, or eggs baked in a little butter or cream.

Sweet Corn and Onion Frittata

1½ tablespoons olive oil
½ large Vidalia (or other really sweet) onion, minced
1 teaspoon cumin seeds
¾ cup fresh corn kernels
4 eggs
Salt and black pepper

Heat the oil in a large nonstick skillet. Add the onion and cumin and sauté gently until the onion is softened. Add the corn and sauté 1 minute. Beat the eggs, season them, and pour into the hot pan. Lower heat, cover the pan with a lid, and cook 3 to 5 minutes until the eggs are set.

Either run the pan under a broiler to cook the top or do the following: Place a plate over the top of the pan. Turn pan and plate upside down so that the omelet falls into the plate, then slide the omelet back into the pan to cook on the bottom side, 2 or 3 minutes. Don't overcook, to keep it creamy not dry.

◆ Serve it in thin wedges for a snack with drinks or wrap it whole in aluminum foil for a picnic, because it keeps its flavor even when cold.

Crab and Avocado Omelet

4 tablespoons butter
1 cup lump crabmeat, well drained
1 ripe avocado, peeled and diced
1 tablespoon fresh lemon juice
½ teaspoon ground cumin
Salt and black and cayenne peppers
1 cup sour cream
6 eggs

In a medium skillet, melt 2 tablespoons of the butter. Add the crab, avocado, lemon juice, cumin, and other seasonings to taste, and heat gently over low heat. Remove from the heat and mix with the sour cream.

Make one omelet at a time in a nonstick skillet (8 to 9 inches is best). Beat the eggs with a fork and season with the salt and peppers. In the skillet, heat 1 tablespoon of the remaining butter over fairly high heat until the butter bubbles and just begins to brown. Add half the eggs, give them 2 seconds to form a film on the bottom of the pan; then, with the back of a fork, push the edges of the cooked eggs toward the middle of the pan to let the unset egg on top contact the hot metal on the bottom (less than a minute).

Spoon half the filling on top of the eggs. Tip the pan away from you over a warm plate and roll the omelet over on itself as you tip it onto the plate. (There's a lot of filling in this omelet and a lot will run out. Don't worry.) Repeat with the remaining butter, eggs, and filling.

◆ Serve with buttered Melba toast and toasted French bread, a leaf-lettuce salad, and fresh figs with triple-cream cheese.

◆ Make a well-seasoned salad of the crab and avocado on a bed of shredded salad greens, surrounded by quartered hard-cooked eggs and green olives. Serve with a mayonnaise spiked with fresh lime juice, mustard, and sherry vinegar or brandy.

◆ Dry Chenin blanc from California or its counterpart, a Vouvray Sec from the Loire, would be best. For brunch, a sparkling Vouvray or Saumur might be even better.

Onion–Cheese Soufflé

1 large onion, minced
4 tablespoons butter
½ cup grated Parmesan cheese
⅛ pound Gorgonzola cheese
¼ pound Fontina cheese
3 eggs, separated
Salt and black pepper

In a small skillet, sauté onion gently in 3 tablespoons of the butter about 8 to 10 minutes, until onion is soft and its liquid has evaporated. With remaining butter, grease inside of a baking dish and sprinkle with 2 tablespoons Parmesan.

Crumble Gorgonzola and grate Fontina coarsely into a large bowl. Add onion and half remaining Parmesan.

In a medium bowl, beat egg yolks, season them, and add to the onion-cheese mixture. In another bowl, beat egg whites until stiff but not dry. Fold whites gently into the mixture and turn all into baking dish. Sprinkle top with the rest of Parmesan. Bake at 400°F. for 20 to 25 minutes and serve immediately (soufflés sink as they cool).

◆ Serve after Roasted Oysters with Curry Butter or Scallops with Hazelnuts.

◆ Instead of a soufflé, make a gratin by layering onion and cheeses with 2 thin-sliced potatoes and a cup of milk or half-and-half. Bake at 350°F. for 50 to 60 minutes, until potatoes are tender.

◆ Forget the rule about "no wine with eggs" and open up a bottle of light red wine, like Valpolicella or Bardolino.

Scallops Seviche

½ pound sea scallops, cut in half crosswise
¼ cup fresh lime juice
¼ cup fresh orange juice
1 small jalapeño or serrano pepper, seeded and diced
1 tablespoon green onion with top, minced
1 tablespoon fresh mint, chopped fine
Salt and black pepper

Put scallops in a glass or porcelain bowl (no metal). Mix the remaining ingredients and pour over the scallops. Cover tightly with plastic wrap and refrigerate about 30 minutes (longer may toughen the scallops).

Roasted Oysters with Curry Butter

2 dozen oysters in the shell
6 tablespoons butter
½ teaspoon Madras curry powder
½ teaspoon minced gingerroot
1 teaspoon fresh lime juice
Salt and black pepper

Preheat oven to 500°F. Crinkle aluminum foil in bottom of a large baking pan to make a nest for the oysters. Place oysters rounded side down in the foil, cover with a large sheet of foil, and seal edges. Roast for 6 to 9 minutes (depending on size), until shells open just enough to pry them apart.

Meanwhile melt butter in a small pan with curry and ginger. Remove pan from the heat and add lime juice. After oysters are roasted and have opened, remove top shells, spoon a little curry butter onto each oyster, season as desired, and serve oysters in their foil nest.

◆ For a special occasion, follow oysters with Venison with Mustard Fruits, accompanied by a green salad. Finish the meal with Dried Apricot Fool.

◆ Roast oysters on an outside grill by covering them with a sheet of foil when coals are ready. Or you can poach shucked oysters in curry butter by melting butter with seasonings in a sauté pan, adding oysters, and gently simmering until their edges just begin to curl.

Chinese Shrimp-in-the-Shell

¾ *pound shrimp*
1 teaspoon salt
½ teaspoon Szechuan peppercorns, ground
½ teaspoon sugar
1 tablespoon each *of minced garlic and gingerroot*
1 green onion with top, minced
1 small fresh red or green chili pepper, seeded and minced
1 cup peanut or vegetable oil

Rinse shrimp, then cut through the shell along outside edge, leaving the shell on. Blot shrimp dry with paper towels. Mix salt, Szechuan pepper, and sugar and set aside. Mix garlic, ginger, onion, and chili pepper and set aside. Heat oil in a wok or deep skillet until smoking hot. Add half the shrimp and fry for 1 minute, then remove with slotted spoon and drain on paper towels. Repeat with remaining shrimp. Discard oil but don't wipe out pan. Place wok over high heat. Add salt mixture and stir for a few seconds, then garlic mixture, then shrimp. Stir-fry for about 2 minutes, turning shrimp to coat on all sides. Serve hot or at room temperature.

◆ Serve shrimp with Chinese Cabbage and Pink Grapefruit Slaw, Honeyed Golden Peppers, or Thai Papaya Salad.

◆ For a different flavor, use the same basic seasonings but smoke the shrimp (see Wok-Smoked Trout, next page). Place shrimp in a single layer over ¼ cup each of tea, brown sugar, and rice, mixed with chili pepper, garlic, ginger, and onion, and smoke for 5 minutes over high heat, then 15 minutes off heat with the lid still on.

Wok–Smoked Trout

2 fresh brook trout
¼ cup each: black tea leaves, brown rice, and brown sugar
A few sprigs fresh thyme, or 1 teaspoon dried thyme
A few sprigs fresh rosemary, or 1 teaspoon dried rosemary
Fresh Italian parsley or cilantro and lemon wedges for garnish

Rinse trout and pat dry. Line a wok with heavy aluminum foil. In the center, mix tea leaves, rice, and sugar, and cover with herbs. Place a rack over the mixture. Line wok lid with foil and cover pan. Set over high heat for about 5 minutes. Remove lid, place trout on rack, leaving space between the 2 fish, then replace lid. Smoke over high heat for 5 minutes. Turn off heat and let wok sit, with lid on, for 15 minutes. Remove lid and serve hot or at room temperature. Garnish trout with fresh Italian parsley or cilantro and serve with a wedge of lemon.

◆ Follow the trout with Gorgonzola Risotto.

◆ Instead of smoking trout, place trout in 2 tablespoons butter with rosemary and thyme in a sealed packet of aluminum foil. Steam in a 350°F. oven for 7 to 10 minutes.

Smoked Haddock Brandade

½ pound smoked haddock (or sable or whitefish)
1 clove garlic, minced
½ cup heavy cream
¼ cup olive oil
Pinch of ground nutmeg
Salt and black and cayenne peppers
Fresh lemon juice to taste

Skin and bone the fish. Put the fish and garlic into a food processor and process until well ground. Heat the cream and oil in separate pans. Add cream to mixture in processor and blend well. While processor is on, add oil slowly through the opening in lid and purée until oil is absorbed. Taste and season with spices and lemon juice.

◆ Serve on toasted slices of French sourdough bread or put purée in the middle of a bowl of mashed potatoes. Brandade is rich in itself and can serve as a full meal with a green salad and a fruit dessert.

◆ Turn similar ingredients into a soup by flaking the fish instead of puréeing, and heating gently with sautéed diced onions and garlic in fish stock (or clam juice) enriched with milk or half-and-half.

Smoked Salmon and Mascarpone Terrine

¼ pound smoked salmon, about 6 thin slices
½ lemon
Black pepper
½ pound mascarpone or triple-cream cheese
2 tablespoons fresh salmon caviar

Overlap 2 slices of smoked salmon in the middle of a piece of plastic wrap in order to make a small rectangle (about 4 inches × 2 inches). Squeeze on a bit of lemon juice, sprinkle with a grinding of black pepper, and spread with a third of the mascarpone. Repeat with remaining slices of salmon and mascarpone to make 2 more layers of salmon with mascarpone on top. Cover top with caviar. Wrap layered "loaf" in the plastic wrap and chill until ready to serve. Cut loaf in half, crosswise.

◆ Serve with thin slices of buttered rye or whole wheat bread or with bagel chips. Or, use as a salad and surround with shredded radicchio or a circle of endive leaves.

◆ Make a pâté by puréeing the salmon in a food processor with the same ingredients, but use only half the amount of mascarpone and garnish with caviar.

Green Chili Soup

1 4-ounce can green chilies (non-pickled)
2 small zucchini, or 1 pattypan squash
3 ears sweet corn (about 2 cups kernels)
3 cups chicken stock
2 tablespoons butter
Salt and black pepper
¼ cup sour cream
Avocado or fresh cilantro for garnish

Dice the chilies (for a milder chili, remove the seeds and veins before dicing). Dice the squash. Remove the corn kernels from the cobs by standing each cob on end and slicing down. Then, with the back of your knife, scrape the cob to get all the corn's "milk."

Put half the chilies and half the corn into a blender and purée. Bring the stock to a boil in a large saucepan and add the purée and zucchini. Simmer for 2 to 3 minutes, or until the squash is almost tender. Add the butter, remaining chilies, corn, and seasonings and simmer for 1 minute. Pour into bowls and top with a dollop of sour cream and diced avocado or chopped cilantro.

◆ Serve with hot buttered tortillas. Follow with sliced mangoes or papaya.

◆ Make a stir-fry with the same vegetables to serve hot or at room temperature. Dice half an onion and sauté it with the zucchini in 2 tablespoons *each* olive oil and butter. Add the chilies and finally the corn. Season well and transfer to a serving bowl. Garnish in the same way as the soup.

◆ A cold rosé with a little sweetness to it will most effectively quench the fire of the chili. Try Rosé d'Anjou, Zinfandel Rosé, or a Chiaretto del Garda from Italy.

Chili-Carrot Soup

1 tablespoon butter or olive oil
¼ pound carrots, sliced
1 small onion, sliced
½ jalapeño pepper, seeded and minced
2 slices gingerroot, minced
2 cups hot chicken stock
½ cup fresh orange juice
Salt and black pepper
1 tablespoon chopped fresh cilantro for garnish

In a medium saucepan, heat butter or oil and gently sauté carrots, onion, jalapeño pepper, and ginger until softened, about 5 minutes. Add stock, cover pan, and simmer 10 minutes, or until vegetables are fork-tender. Purée mixture in a blender and return liquid to pan. Add orange juice, taste and adjust seasoning, and bring to the simmer. If soup is too thick, add more stock. Garnish with cilantro.

◆ Serve hot or cold, with papadums or toasted bialys.

◆ Instead of orange juice, add a large ripe tomato, seeded and chopped, to the vegetables in the saucepan. Or simply add ½ cup tomato juice. To turn soup into a carrot purée for a vegetable garnish, double the amount of carrots and diminish the total liquid to 1 cup: ¾ cup stock, ¼ cup orange juice.

Red Pepper–Garlic Soup

2 tablespoons olive oil
2 sweet red peppers, seeded and chopped
10 cloves garlic, mashed
1 cup chicken or fish stock
½ to 1 teaspoon balsamic vinegar
Salt and black pepper
4 fresh sage leaves for garnish

In a medium skillet, heat oil and sauté peppers and garlic over moderately high heat for 1 or 2 minutes. Add stock, bring to the boil, cover, and simmer gently for about 15 minutes or until vegetables are soft. Purée vegetables with the liquid in a blender. Add vinegar and seasoning. Garnish soup with sage.

◆ Serve with a crusty French or Italian loaf or with Roast Potato Chips and an Orange-Onion-Basil Salad with Tahini Dressing.

◆ Change the soup to a sauce by using only ¼ cup liquid, or just enough to make a purée. This sauce is particularly good on linguine, spaghettini, or a grilled fish.

Corn and Sorrel Soup

1 tablespoon butter or olive oil
1½ cups sorrel leaves, packed
3 cups chicken stock
2 ears sweet corn, kernels cut off, about 1½ cups
Salt and black pepper
Fresh basil leaves or dill for garnish

In a medium saucepan, heat butter or oil, add sorrel leaves and wilt over low heat. Add stock and bring liquid to the boil. Put corn kernels in a blender, add sorrel soup, and purée (easier to do in 2 batches). Add seasoning. Garnish bowls with basil, dill, or other fresh herbs. This soup is good hot or cold.

◆ Serve with a hefty salad like Mussels in Hot Potato Salad or Hot Bacon and Egg Salad.

◆ Instead of sorrel, use tender greens such as mustard, turnip, or dandelion. For a creamier texture, use 2½ cups stock and 1 cup buttermilk or half-and-half.

Daikon and Mint Soup

1 tablespoon olive oil
¾ cup chopped onion
¾ cup peeled and chopped daikon
1½ cups chicken stock
¾ cup plain yogurt
3 tablespoons chopped fresh mint leaves
Salt and black pepper

In a medium skillet, heat oil and sauté onion and daikon for 2 or 3 minutes, or until softened. Add stock, bring to a boil, then purée mixture in a blender. Add yogurt and half of the mint, blend, and taste and adjust seasoning. Pour soup into bowls and garnish with remaining mint leaves. Good hot or cold.

◆ Make a full meal with a bowl of Red Lentils or an Onion-Cheese Soufflé.

◆ Steamed daikon is delicate and delicious. Dice or cut it lengthwise into strips like carrot strips, then steam for 3 or 4 minutes. Toss in melted butter or mix with yogurt flavored with sautéed onion and chopped mint.

Orange–Cranberry Soup

1½ tablespoons butter
3 green onions with tops, chopped
1½ cups chicken stock
¾ cup cranberries
2 oranges
2 tablespoons dry sherry

In a small saucepan, heat butter and sauté onions for 2 or 3 minutes, until soft. Add broth and cranberries, bring to the simmer, and cook gently for 5 to 6 minutes, until cranberries pop. Purée mixture in a blender. Cut the oranges in half. Cut 2 thin slices from one of the halves for garnish and squeeze remaining oranges for juice to get ¾ cup. Add juice and sherry to cranberry purée. If serving soup hot, reheat liquid gently for a moment or two. Otherwise, chill liquid until ready for use. Garnish each bowl with a slice of orange.

◆ Serve as a starter for a dish of Turkey Scallopini or for grilled quail or roast chicken.

◆ Use beets instead of cranberries for a darker red and slightly sweeter soup. Balance the sweetness of beets by adding a little fresh lemon juice or a dash of sherry vinegar instead of dry sherry.

White Bean and Burnt Almond Soup

⅓ cup slivered almonds
2 tablespoons butter
1 onion, chopped
2 tablespoons fresh cilantro, chopped
2 cloves garlic, mashed
Salt and black and cayenne peppers
1 cup white kidney beans, cooked or canned
3 cups hot chicken stock
Cilantro sprigs for garnish

In a large skillet, brown the almonds in the butter until well toasted, remove and reserve. In the same skillet sauté the onion until it begins to brown, then add the remaining ingredients, including the almonds. Cover the pan and simmer about 5 minutes. Pour the mixture into a blender and purée until smooth. Thin with more stock if needed. Garnish each bowl with a sprig of cilantro.

◆ Instead of a soup, you can make a dip of this mixture by omitting the chicken stock and puréeing the sautéed onions, almonds, garlic, seasonings, and beans in a food processor.

Salads

Orange, Radish, and Olive Salad
Eggplant Salad with Yogurt Dressing
Roasted Pepper Salad
Hot Bacon and Egg Salad
Brie-Arugula Salad with Balsamic Cream Dressing
Thai Papaya Salad
Hot Beet Salad
Tropical Fruit Salad
Orange-Onion-Basil Salad with Tahini Dressing
Sweet Corn Salad with Cucumber Dressing
Hot Pear Salad in Chinese Hot Sauce
Crisped Chicory and Hominy Salad

Orange, Radish, and Olive Salad

2 navel oranges, peeled and sliced
6 red radishes, tops and roots removed
6 black Mediterranean-cured olives, pitted
1 tablespoon olive oil
¼ teaspoon ground cumin
⅛ teaspoon cinnamon
Black pepper

Layer the orange slices in a bowl. Slice the radishes paper thin and place them on the oranges. Top with the olives, cut into slivers. Mix the oil with the seasonings and dribble it over the top of the salad.

◆ Oranges with cinnamon spell Morocco, and for another Moroccan salad, mix fresh oranges with grated carrots and a little sugar, cinnamon, and orange blossom water.

Eggplant Salad with Yogurt Dressing

2 to 3 tablespoons olive oil
2 unpeeled Japanese eggplants, quartered lengthwise and diced
1 medium tomato, seeded and diced
½ teaspoon ground cumin
2 tablespoons fresh mint leaves, chopped fine
Salt and black and cayenne peppers

DRESSING:
2 large cloves garlic, skins on
2 tablespoons olive oil
¼ cup plain yogurt
1 tablespoon fresh lemon juice
Salt and black pepper

Heat the oil in a heavy skillet and when it is very hot, add the diced eggplant, turning the cubes to brown on all sides quickly before they get soft. Remove to a bowl and immediately mix with the tomato, cumin, mint, and seasonings. Cover and let cool to room temperature.

For the dressing, dry-roast the garlic in a skillet until the skins blacken in spots. When cool enough to handle, remove the skins and put the garlic into a blender with the other ingredients. Blend until smooth. Pour the dressing over the eggplant.

Roasted Pepper Salad

2 sweet red peppers
2 small zucchini
¼ pound feta cheese, drained and rinsed
1 small bunch fresh spinach
¼ pound Monterey Jack or Muenster cheese
2 teaspoons balsamic vinegar
⅓ cup olive oil
Salt and black pepper

Char the skins of the red peppers under a broiler or directly over a gas flame. Remove the skins, stems, and seeds. Cut the flesh into strips lengthwise.

Don't peel the zucchini but cut off both ends. Shred the zucchini in a processor, or cut in fine strips lengthwise; then mix with the crumbled feta.

Cut off the spinach stems, wash the leaves well, and spin them dry. Make a bed of the spinach on a serving plate. Arrange the peppers with strips of Monterey Jack cheese in a sunburst pattern on the spinach. Put the zucchini in the middle.

Make a dressing by mixing together the vinegar, oil, and seasonings and pour over the salad.

Hot Bacon and Egg Salad

2 large eggs
6 thick slices bacon
2 teaspoons balsamic vinegar
Salt and black pepper
1 bunch watercress, arugula, New Zealand spinach, or escarole, etc.

Cover eggs with cold water in a small pan, bring to the boil, cover, and remove from heat. Let sit for 20 minutes, then run eggs under cold water before peeling.

Fry bacon until crisp, remove, and cut in small pieces. Pour off all but 3 tablespoons of fat. Mix fat with vinegar and seasonings.

Clean greens and put in a salad bowl. Peel and slice eggs and arrange over the greens. Sprinkle bacon over eggs and pour fat and vinegar mixture over top.

◆ Serve with Chili-Carrot Soup or Smoked Haddock Brandade.

◆ Another version of this salad is to add fried and chopped bacon to 3 beaten eggs, then fry eggs in a tablespoon of fat, turning them once. Turn eggs onto a plate, cut "omelet" in thin slices, and add to greens. Use a bacon-fat dressing as above.

Brie-Arugula Salad with Balsamic Cream Dressing

1 bunch arugula
⅓ pound ripe Brie

DRESSING:
⅓ cup olive oil
½ egg, beaten
1 teaspoon balsamic vinegar
Salt and black pepper

Wash and dry arugula and arrange in a salad bowl.

Cut off rind of cheese and cut cheese into cubes. Mix with arugula.

Purée ingredients for dressing in a blender and pour over salad.

◆ With arugula or other greens, cube Brie or other cheeses such as goat cheese, Gruyère, Monterey Jack. Toss cubes in bread crumbs and sauté quickly in olive oil. Add to salad.

Thai Papaya Salad

1 ripe papaya
1 jalapeño pepper, minced
2 ripe tomatoes, seeded and chopped
6 snow peas, cut diagonally in slivers
¼ cup peanut oil
1 to 2 tablespoons fresh lime juice
1 teaspoon brown sugar
½ teaspoon anchovy paste
⅓ cup roasted peanuts, chopped

Cut papaya in quarters, peel and remove seeds. Cut in thin slices lengthwise and arrange them on a platter.

Mix jalapeño, tomatoes, and snow peas and sprinkle over papaya.

Combine oil, lime juice, sugar, and anchovy paste, taste for seasoning and adjust. Pour dressing over salad and garnish with peanuts.

◆ Serve with Picadillo or Star-Anise Beef with Snow Peas.

◆ Cut papaya into cubes and toss with shrimp, crisply fried and chopped, and mix with same seasonings.

Hot Beet Salad

1 bunch of young beets with tops
½ red onion, sliced thin
4 tablespoons olive oil
1 tablespoon red wine vinegar
Salt and black pepper
¼ cup walnuts, chopped
2 tablespoons chopped fresh mint leaves

Cut off tops 1 inch above beets. In a medium saucepan, boil beets with their skins on in boiling water to cover, about 30 to 45 minutes, or until tender. Drain and run under cold water so that you can slip off their skins. Slice beets thin.

Sauté onion in oil in a small skillet to soften slightly. Remove from heat, then add vinegar, seasonings, walnuts, and mint and pour dressing over beets.

◆ A good salad for the Tuscan Liver Sauté or the Beef and Wild Mushroom Sauté.

◆ For a cold beet salad, try a dressing of sour cream seasoned with lime and fresh dill and sprinkled with walnuts.

Tropical Fruit Salad

2 Belgian endives
½ red papaya
1 mango, or ¼ fresh pineapple
1 avocado
1 blood orange
1 Chinese starfruit

DRESSING:
⅓ cup olive oil
2 to 3 tablespoons fresh lime or lemon juice
1 tablespoon honey
½ to 1 teaspoon New Mexican ground chili
Salt and black pepper

Arrange the leaves of endive on a round platter and layer the fruit on top, beginning with slivers of papaya, mango, and avocado, then crosswise slices of orange and starfruit.

Mix together all the ingredients of the dressing and pour it over the top.

◆ This is a meal for any time of day or night, using any number of tropical fruits and fresh greens. Jícama, avocado, and pineapple go well together on a bed of arugula or frisée.

Orange–Onion–Basil Salad with Tahini Dressing

2 navel oranges
1 medium red or Vidalia onion
2 or 3 radicchio leaves, shredded
6 to 8 fresh basil leaves, shredded

DRESSING:
¼ teaspoon soy sauce
Salt and black pepper
1 clove garlic, mashed
2 teaspoons sesame oil
1 tablespoon tahini paste
2 tablespoons orange juice
Fresh lemon juice or vinegar to taste

Peel oranges, remove white pith, and slice thinly. Slice onion very thin and alternate orange and onion slices on a bed of shredded radicchio. Sprinkle with shredded basil leaves.

Combine ingredients for dressing with a fork or small whisk. If mixture is too stiff, add more orange juice or a little white wine. Pour dressing over salad.

◆ Serve with Fresh Corn Tamale Pie.

◆ Use same dressing for salad greens such as endive, slivered Chinese cabbage, or steamed bok choy.

Sweet Corn Salad with Cucumber Dressing

4 ears sweet corn, kernels cut off (about 3 cups)
1 sweet red pepper, seeded and chopped
2 large red leaf-lettuce leaves

DRESSING:
¼ cup seeded and chopped cucumber
1 tablespoon fresh dill
¼ small fresh red or green chili pepper
1 teaspoon fresh lemon juice
1 teaspoon olive oil
⅓ cup plain yogurt
Salt and black pepper
Dill sprigs for garnish

Mix corn and red pepper and place on lettuce leaves.

Purée ingredients for dressing in a blender. Taste for seasoning and adjust. Pour dressing over salad and garnish with a few sprigs of dill.

◆ A good summer salad to go with any grilled fish or fowl.

◆ If raw corn is too raw for you, boil (or grill) the ears for 1 to 3 minutes with their husks on, remove husks, and cut off the kernels. Mix with whatever vegetables you choose.

Hot Pear Salad in Chinese Hot Sauce

2 firm Bosc pears
½ small fresh red chili pepper
½ clove garlic, minced
2 slices gingerroot, peeled and shredded
2 tablespoons sesame oil

Quarter and peel the pears and cut into thick slices. Sauté the pepper, garlic, and gingerroot in the oil for 2 to 3 minutes. Add the pears and brown them quickly on both sides.

◆ This makes a good salad served at room temperature on a couple of red lettuce leaves. It is also a good accompaniment, hot or warm, for roast birds or pork.

Crisped Chicory and Hominy Salad

Oil for deep frying
1 small bunch chicory, washed and dried
1 cup canned hominy, drained
Salt and black pepper

In a medium skillet, heat the oil until hot but not smoking. Make sure the chicory leaves are well dried, then fry them a few at a time until they are very crispy. Drain on paper towels. Mix them with the hominy kernels and season to taste.

◆ Deep-fried parsley or deep-fried sea vegetables (formerly called seaweeds) also go extremely well with hominy's earthy taste and texture.

Vegetables

Ricotta Greens
Kale and Red Pepper Sauté
Chinese Greens with Pesto
Fresh Corn Tamale Pie
Dated Carrots
Bok Choy and Carrots
Parsnip Purée
Sautéed Escarole
Broccoli and Cauliflowerets
Tahini Broccoli
Wok-Grilled Fennel
Zucchini Gratin
Eggplant Torta
Sesame Eggplant
Appled Eggplant
Honeyed Golden Peppers
Turnip-Pear Purée
Chinese Cabbage and Pink Grapefruit Slaw
Pesto Spaghetti Squash
Pan-Grilled Portobello Mushrooms
Apricot Sweet Potatoes
Sweet Potato Stir-Fry
Garlic Roast Potatoes
Mahogany Potatoes
Potatoes Poblano
Bacon and Potato Pancake
Mashed Potatoes Tapenade
Braised Onions and Lemons
Lentil-Plantain-Pineapple Ragout

Ricotta Greens

1 pound mixed greens (dandelion, mustard, turnip, curly endive, or
    watercress)
1 small onion, minced
1 clove garlic, minced
2 tablespoons olive oil
1 cup ricotta cheese
½ cup grated Parmesan cheese
½ cup heavy cream
2 eggs, beaten
1 to 2 tablespoons fresh lemon juice
4 sprigs fresh mint or basil
Salt and black and cayenne peppers

Cut off and discard the stems; then wash the greens well.

In a large skillet with a lid, sauté the onion and garlic in the oil briefly. Add the greens, cover, and cook over low heat until the greens are tender, 10 to 20 minutes, depending on the greens. Drain, chop coarsely, drain again, and save juice for another purpose, such as soup.

Purée the remaining ingredients in a blender or processor and mix with the greens in a buttered baking dish. Cover with a lid or aluminum foil and bake at 325°F. for 20 to 30 minutes, or until the eggs are set.

◆ Serve with smoked capon, smoked fish, or delicatessen meats like prosciutto.

◆ Serve the same greens as a salad with a hot dressing. Cut 2 or 3 thick slices of smoked bacon into strips and fry until crisp. Sprinkle them over the chopped raw greens. Add 2 teaspoons wine vinegar to 2 tablespoons hot fat and pour over the greens.

◆ A fairly tart white is required to play off the bitterness of the greens. Try Sancerre or Pouilly Fumé from the Loire, Premier Cru Chablis, white Graves, or a California Sauvignon Blanc.

Kale and Red Pepper Sauté

1 bunch young kale
1 sweet red pepper
2 tablespoons olive oil
½ red onion, chopped
2 cloves garlic, minced
Salt and cayenne pepper, or red pepper flakes

Wash kale, cut off stems, and chop leaves finely, crosswise.

Seed pepper and cut it in eighths lengthwise, then cut strips diagonally into triangles. In a large skillet, sauté pepper in oil over high heat to char triangles slightly on both sides.

Lower heat and sauté onion and garlic for 2 or 3 minutes.

Add kale and ¼ cup water to the pan. Season, lower heat, and cook, covered, for 8 to 10 minutes, or until kale is tender but still crunchy.

◆ Serve along with Honey-Mustard Spareribs.

◆ For a one-dish meal, add a handful of young fava or lima beans to the vegetables, together with diced ham or crumbled bacon.

Chinese Greens with Pesto

1 small Chinese cabbage
1 small bunch spinach leaves
3 or 4 red radishes

PESTO:
⅓ cup basil leaves (packed)
2 tablespoons chopped fresh parsley
1 clove garlic, mashed
¼ cup peanut oil
2 teaspoons sesame oil
1 tablespoon sherry
1 teaspoon soy sauce
Rice wine (optional)

Slice cabbage very thin crosswise, to make 3 or 4 cups.

Wash spinach thoroughly and spin-dry. Bunch leaves and shred finely with a knife or scissors.

Clean and slice radishes. Mix with the spinach and cabbage in a bowl.

Purée ingredients for sauce in a blender. If mixture is too thick, add a little rice wine. Toss sauce with the mixed greens.

◆ A good salad for Pork in Plum Sauce or Duck Breasts with Black Bean Sauce.

◆ Use the same dressing for a salad of chopped bok choy or grilled Japanese eggplant.

Fresh Corn Tamale Pie

6 ears sweet corn, kernels cut off (about 4 to 5 cups)
Salt and black pepper
1 small onion, chopped
2 cloves garlic, minced
1 tablespoon oil
⅓ pound ground pork
¼ cup raisins
¼ cup stuffed green olives, chopped
2 poblano chilies, roasted, seeded, and chopped
½ teaspoon each *of ground cumin and oregano*

Purée corn kernels, with salt and pepper, in a blender. Butter a small loaf pan and put half the corn purée in bottom.

In a medium skillet, sauté onion and garlic in the oil until softened. Add pork and brown it lightly. Add raisins, olives, chilies, cumin, and oregano and sauté for 2 or 3 minutes.

Spread mixture over bottom layer of corn in loaf pan and cover it with remaining corn purée. Cover pan tightly with foil and bake at 350°F. for about 30 minutes.

◆ Serve with Orange-Onion-Basil Salad with Tahini Dressing and end with Papaya-Tomato Compote.

◆ If you lack fresh corn, use ½ cup cornmeal cooked in 1½ cups chicken or beef stock (soften the meal first in ½ cup cold water, then stir in the boiling stock). Cook cornmeal in a double boiler about 30 minutes, stirring often, then pour half into buttered pan, add pork filling, and cover pork with remaining cornmeal. Bake as above.

◆ Try this wine-versatile dish with Blanc de Blancs sparkling wines, light, fruity red wines like Beaujolais, or fruity California Chardonnays.

Dated Carrots

1 tablespoon butter
2 cups fresh carrots (slivere, sliced or whole baby carrots)
1 dozen dried dates, pitted
2 cups chicken stock
1 teaspoon garam masala, or similar Indian or Middle Eastern spice mix
Salt and black pepper
Fresh lemon juice to taste

Heat the butter in a large heavy saucepan and brown the carrots quickly. Add the dates, chicken stock, spice, and seasonings, and bring to the boil. Cover the pan and simmer 10 to 15 minutes, or until the carrots are tender. Add lemon to taste to balance the sweetness of the dates.

◆ This is a particularly good accompaniment for lamb, pork, or game.

Bok Choy and Carrots

2 tablespoons olive oil
3 carrots, sliced thin
1 teaspoon fennel seeds
1 small bok choy, sliced thin crosswise
Salt and black pepper

Heat the olive oil in a heavy or nonstick skillet. Add the carrots and brown them quickly over high heat, with the fennel, for 2 to 3 minutes. Add the bok choy and seasonings and sauté for no more than 2 minutes to keep the vegetables crisp.

◆ To turn this into a main dish, add thin strips of veal scallops to brown with the carrots and fennel.

Parsnip Purée

1 pound parsnips
4 tablespoons butter
¼ to ½ cup buttermilk
Salt and black pepper
Nutmeg

Peel and dice the parsnips. Put them in a large skillet with water to cover and boil them until tender, about 5 minutes. Drain them in a colander and put them in a food processor. Add the remaining ingredients, adding the buttermilk gradually until you have the thickness you want.

Sautéed Escarole

½ head escarole
1 or 2 cloves garlic, minced
½ small onion, chopped fine
1 jalapeño or other chili pepper, seeded and minced
2 tablespoons olive oil
Salt and black pepper

Wash and spin-dry the escarole leaves. Bunch together and cut crosswise into 1-inch segments.

Sauté garlic, onion, and jalapeño in oil in a medium skillet for 1 or 2 minutes. Add escarole and seasonings and sauté about 5 minutes or until escarole is somewhat wilted.

◆ Serve as a companion for Roasted Garlic Cod or Steamed Clams with Vegetables.

◆ Sautéed escarole is a fine bitter accent for pasta in the same way that broccoli rabe is. As a green, escarole would also substitute well for the rabe in Squab and Rabe.

Broccoli and Cauliflowerets

½ small head broccoli
½ small head cauliflower
½ small dried chili pepper, crushed
½ teaspoon mustard seeds
¼ teaspoon cardamom seeds, crushed
⅛ teaspoon mace
Salt and black pepper
¼ cup sesame oil

Cut the flowerets of the broccoli and cauliflower from their stems. (Reserve the stems for another purpose, such as soup.) Mix the spices together. Put the vegetables in a steamer (or in a colander set in a pot of boiling water with a lid), sprinkle on the spices, cover, and steam for 5 to 7 minutes until tender but crisp. Transfer to a serving platter and dribble the oil over the top.

Tahini Broccoli

1 pound broccoli
1 tablespoon olive oil
1 tablespoon tahini
2 tablespoons boiling water
1 tablespoon fresh lemon juice
Salt and black pepper

Cut off tough ends of broccoli stems and remove outer leaves. Cut off flowerets with their stems and peel off any tough skin from stems.

Drop broccoli into a large saucepan full of boiling salted water and boil for about 3 minutes, or until just tender. Drain.

Put oil and tahini in a bowl and pour in boiling water, stirring until mixture is smooth. Add lemon juice and seasonings. Pour sauce on a plate and arrange broccoli on top.

◆ Good for a Beef and Wild Mushroom Sauté or Onion-Cheese Soufflé.

◆ For a broccoli purée, proceed as above, only purée the boiled broccoli with the tahini and seasonings in a food processor. A tahini dressing also does well with broccoli rabe or other bitter greens, such as mustard, kale, or collards.

Wok-Grilled Fennel

1 head fennel
2 tablespoons olive oil
1 teaspoon balsamic vinegar

Cut a thin slice off root end of fennel and cut off top stalks. Cut head in half lengthwise and then into ½-inch slices lengthwise.

Heat wok until almost smoking, add oil, then fennel. Char slices on both sides, turning frequently. Sprinkle with vinegar and serve hot or at room temperature.

◆ Fennel goes especially well with fish and chicken.

◆ For a one-dish meal, grill fennel with strips of sweet red pepper or chili poblano, red onions, zucchini, and eggplant. Mix with black Mediterranean olives and strips of seared tuna or swordfish.

Zucchini Gratin

1 pound small zucchini
2 tablespoons olive oil
½ cup wheat germ
½ teaspoon dried oregano
Salt and black and cayenne peppers

Remove the stem ends of the zucchini but leave the skins on. Shred in a processor. Add 1 teaspoon of salt and let the zucchini drain for 10 minutes. Rinse and pat dry with paper towels. Put in a shallow buttered baking pan and sprinkle with the olive oil, wheat germ, and seasonings. Bake at 450°F. for 15 minutes. Serve at any temperature.

Eggplant Torta

½ pound eggplant
1 large onion
2 ripe tomatoes
Salt, black pepper, and dried oregano
¼ cup olive oil
¾ cup ricotta cheese
1 clove garlic, minced
¼ cup fresh Italian parsley, chopped
⅛ pound mozzarella, sliced
¼ cup grated Parmesan cheese

Slice the eggplant into ¼-inch-thick slices and place on top of aluminum foil on a broiling rack. Slice the onion the same thickness. Cut the tomatoes in half and squeeze out the seeds. Put the onion and tomatoes, cut side up, on the same broiling rack. Season the vegetables with salt, pepper, and oregano and drizzle the oil over the top. Broil for 3 to 5 minutes, or until the tops are browned.

Mix the ricotta with the garlic and parsley. In a baking dish, place half the eggplant, browned side up, in a single layer on the bottom, and top with half the onion slices and tomatoes. (Press the tomatoes flat with a fork.) Cover with the ricotta and half the mozzarella. Layer the remaining tomatoes, onions, and eggplant, browned side down, and top with the remaining mozzarella and the Parmesan. Bake at 350°F. for 25 to 35 minutes.

◆ Serve with shrimp and Tapenade Dip to start, and end with sweet red seedless grapes.

◆ Make a ratatouille by frying the onion, garlic, cubed eggplant, sweet red and green peppers, zucchini, and tomatoes in olive oil and chopped herbs. Add a crumbled poached Italian sausage, such as cotechino, or cubed fried sweet or hot Italian sausages, together with pitted black olives.

◆ A good medium-bodied Zinfandel, such as Sutter Home, will do well here, or a Chianti Classico. For something slightly different, a Bandol (look for Domaine Tempier) from Provence would be an excellent choice.

Sesame Eggplant

2 Japanese eggplants (long and narrow)
½ cup sesame seeds
Salt and black pepper
¼ cup olive oil

Cut off the stem ends of the eggplants. Cut lengthwise into quarters or eighths and then in half to make eggplant fingers. Sprinkle with salt and let drain for 10 minutes.

Meanwhile, toast the sesame seeds at 375°F. oven for 5 to 8 minutes. Remove. Raise the oven temperature to 450°F. Pat the eggplant dry with paper towels, sprinkle them with pepper, and roll them quickly in the olive oil. Put them in a baking pan and bake for 8 to 10 minutes, or until just tender. Coat with the sesame seeds and serve.

Appled Eggplant

1 large Japanese eggplant
1 tart green apple
½ teaspoon salt
¼ teaspoon ground fennel seeds
¼ teaspoon turmeric
⅛ teaspoon cayenne pepper
1 tablespoon water
4 tablespoons vegetable oil

Cut eggplant crosswise into ½-inch slices.

Cut apple (leave peel on) into eighths and remove core.

Mix seasonings with a tablespoon of water.

In a large skillet, brown apple slices quickly in oil over high heat and remove them. Brown eggplant slices quickly in same oil. Return apples to the skillet, add seasonings, turn heat very low, cover pan, and cook for about 10 minutes, or until the eggplant is tender.

◆ Serve with roast pork or lamb or Turkey Scallopini.

◆ For a variant on the apple-eggplant combo, bake a regular eggplant with a whole cored apple and an onion at 400°F. for about 50 minutes, or until eggplant is soft. Scrape eggplant pulp into a food processor, add apple, salt, and a cup of plain yogurt and purée. Chop onion and add to purée.

Honeyed Golden Peppers

2 sweet golden peppers
2 tablespoons dark honey
1 tablespoon balsamic vinegar
Salt and black pepper
1 tablespoon butter, melted

Stem peppers, cut in half, and remove seeds. Cut each half in strips lengthwise.

Stir honey, vinegar, and seasonings into butter in a skillet and heat. Pour sauce over peppers and serve.

◆ A colorful addition to Black Pepper Salmon Steaks or a roast bird.

◆ Turn the same ingredients into a sauce for a pork loin or chicken breasts. Simply purée peppers after cooking them in the sauce for about 10 minutes.

Turnip–Pear Purée

1 large or 2 small turnips
1 ripe pear
2 tablespoons butter
¼ teaspoon mace, or ground nutmeg
Salt and white and cayenne peppers
Fresh lemon juice to taste
4 to 5 green onions with tops, chopped fine

Peel turnip, cut it into quarters, and drop into a medium saucepan full of boiling water to cook until tender, about 8 to 10 minutes. Drain and put turnip into a food processor.

Cut pear into quarters, remove peel and core, and in a small skillet sauté pear quickly in butter and mace. Put pear in processor with remaining seasonings and lemon juice. Purée until smooth.

Sauté onions for 1 to 2 minutes and stir into purée.

◆ A delicate companion for Scallops with Hazelnuts or Barbados Chicken.

◆ Turnip-apple is another good combination, especially when the apple is sautéed in a little bacon fat from bacon that you crumble over the top of the purée when done.

Chinese Cabbage and Pink Grapefruit Slaw

1 small Chinese cabbage
1 pink grapefruit
⅓ cup vinaigrette, or other dressing

Shred cabbage finely to yield 3 or 4 cups. Place in a bowl.

Peel and remove pith of the grapefruit. Segment and remove outer membranes. Place segments on cabbage and pour on vinaigrette or other salad dressing.

◆ This is a very crisp and refreshing accompaniment to a rich dish such as Honey-Mustard Spareribs or Pork in Plum Sauce.

◆ Make a sweet-and-sour slaw of Chinese cabbage by tossing it with vinegar, sugar, minced hot chilies, ginger, and sesame oil.

Pesto Spaghetti Squash

½ spaghetti squash, cut lengthwise
2 tablespoons olive oil

YOGURT-PESTO:
2 tablespoons olive oil
⅓ cup plain yogurt
⅔ cup basil leaves, packed
3 tablespoons chopped fresh parsley
½ teaspoon salt
1 large clove garlic, mashed
2 tablespoons pine nuts, toasted
2 tablespoons grated Parmesan cheese

Remove seeds from cut squash, brush flat surface with olive oil and place cut-side down in baking pan. Bake at 400°F. for 40 to 50 minutes, or until fork-tender.

Put all the ingredients for pesto, except cheese, into a blender and purée until smooth. If mixture is too thick, add boiling water or chicken stock. Remove sauce to a bowl and stir in cheese.

With a fork, shred squash into spaghetti-like strands and pour pesto over top.

◆ This can be a meal in itself, like pasta and pesto, or can be a fit companion for a soup or a stir-fry.

◆ This comically versatile squash is also delicious with a poblano sauce (see Charred Shrimp Poblano) or pumpkin-seed sauce (see Pumpkin-Seed Quail). Or, treat it like a real pasta and toss it with clams, garlic, and parsley or a *gremolata* of grated lemon rind, garlic, and parsley.

Pan-Grilled Portobello Mushrooms

2 large portobello mushrooms
⅓ cup olive oil
2 cloves garlic, minced
1 tablespoon fresh rosemary, or 1 teaspoon dried rosemary
1 teaspoon fresh thyme, or ½ teaspoon dried thyme
Salt and black pepper

Remove the stems from the mushrooms and wipe off the top of each mushroom with a damp paper towel. Make a marinade of the remaining ingredients and pour it over the mushrooms (they'll soak it up).

Heat a griddle or heavy skillet until very hot. Sear the mushrooms on both sides, lower the heat, and grill until the mushrooms are just fork-tender, about 5 to 7 minutes.

◆ Serve by itself as a salad or main dish, or slice it and serve as a companion dish.

Apricot Sweet Potatoes

½ cup dried apricots
¾ cup boiling water
1 large or 2 small sweet potatoes
½ cup plain yogurt or sour cream
Salt and black pepper
Juice of ½ lemon
¼ cup candied ginger, diced

In a small bowl, cover apricots with boiling water and let soak.

In a small saucepan, boil sweet potato in its skin for 20 to 30 minutes, or until fork-tender. Cool, peel, and chunk the potato into a processor.

Add apricots and their liquid to the processor, together with yogurt, seasonings, and lemon juice, and purée until smooth. Stir in candied ginger or use it for a garnish.

◆ Serve with roast venison or turkey or any game.

◆ Other dried fruits, such as apples, currants, or pears, will enhance the inherent sweetness of sweet potatoes; yams or squashes such as acorn or butternut are all good for puréeing.

Sweet Potato Stir-Fry

1 small sweet potato
1 small onion, thinly sliced
1 sweet red pepper, sliced lengthwise
4 tablespoons butter
1 tart apple (Granny Smith)
1 tablespoon fresh lemon juice
¼ teaspoon mace
Salt and black pepper

In a small saucepan, boil the sweet potato in its skin until barely tender. Peel and slice; then cut the slices into strips. In a medium skillet, sauté the onion and red pepper in the butter. Peel, core, and slice the apple and add it to the onion. Add the sweet potato, lemon juice, and seasonings, sauté quickly over high heat, and serve.

Garlic Roast Potatoes

1 pound new potatoes
6 cloves garlic
2 sprigs fresh rosemary, or 1 teaspoon dried rosemary
Salt and black pepper
4 tablespoons butter

Wash the potatoes and place them on a large square of aluminum foil. Peel the garlic and add the cloves to the potatoes. Sprinkle with the rosemary leaves and salt and pepper. Dot with the butter. Bring up the edges of the foil to make a sealed packet and bake at 425°F. for 45 to 50 minutes if the potatoes are medium size, 25 to 30 minutes if they are small. Keep the potatoes hot in the packet until ready to serve.

Mahogany Potatoes

2 medium baking potatoes, peeled and sliced very thin
6 tablespoons butter
Salt and black pepper

Because you need to overlap the slices in a *single* layer, you need to use either two 8-inch skillets or one 12-inch skillet, and they should be either nonstick or well-seasoned pans. Butter the bottom of each pan well with 3 tablespoons of butter. Overlap the potatoes in a circle until you cover the bottom of each pan and sprinkle with the seasonings. Cover each pan and cook over low heat about 30 minutes, until the bottoms are browned. Put the pans in a 200°F. oven to finish drying and crisping the tops. The potatoes will turn a beautiful mahogany brown.

◆ This is a lazy man's Potatoes Anna. You can eat the potatoes right out of the pan or slide the whole thing onto a platter. I count one potato per person, but if you're less greedy you can count one per two.

Potatoes Poblano

1 pound new potatoes, yellow Finns, or Peruvian blues
½ medium onion
4 cloves garlic, skins on
2 poblano chilies, roasted, skinned, seeded, and chopped
2 tablespoons fresh cilantro
1 tablespoon olive oil
⅓ to ½ cup chicken stock
Salt

In a medium saucepan, boil the potatoes in salted water to cover until tender. Drain well.

Pan-grill the onion and garlic in a heavy cast-iron skillet until both are slightly charred. Remove the skins from the garlic. Put the onion, garlic, and roasted chilies into a blender, with the remaining ingredients, and purée to make a sauce with a pesto-like consistency. Add more stock if the purée is too thick.

Pour the sauce over the potatoes and serve hot or cold.

◆ Any leftovers the next day can be turned into a really good soup by puréeing the potatoes with the sauce and adding more chicken or vegetable stock to thin the mixture. If you can get any, add the magnificent Mexican herb called *hoja santa*, or some arugula, for added color and flavor.

Bacon and Potato Pancake

8 slices bacon, or 1 cup pork, duck, or chicken cracklings
2 large Idaho potatoes
4 tablespoons bacon or beef fat
2 green onions with tops, chopped
¼ cup minced parsley
¼ teaspoon dried thyme
Salt and black pepper

Snip the bacon crosswise into ¼-inch strips and fry in a large skillet. Remove the bacon to paper towels with a slotted spoon and pour off all but 4 tablespoons of fat.

Scrub the potatoes and grate them, skin and all, in a processor or by hand. Heat the fat in the skillet over high heat and spread the potatoes to cover the bottom of the pan. Sprinkle the potatoes with onions, bacon, parsley, and seasonings. Flatten the pancake with a spatula to mix in the garnishes and get a good crust. Turn the heat to medium.

When the bottom of the pancake is well browned, slide it onto a large plate, invert the skillet over the plate and turn right-side up so that the uncooked side of the pancake is on the bottom of the skillet. Brown the bottom of the pancake for 5 to 8 minutes, and slip it onto a serving plate. Cut into quarters to serve.

◆ Serve with Broccoli and Cauliflowerets and follow with ripe melon sprinkled with salt and lime.

◆ Make a pastrami hash. Dice ¼ pound pastrami (or corned beef) and add to the grated potatoes, onions, and parsley. Add a mashed anchovy for salt. Fry in beef or chicken fat, if possible.

◆ Try a useful dry white, like a Mâcon-Villages or a dry Orvieto, or California Pinot Blanc. If you prefer red, a Beaujolais-Villages would be fine.

Mashed Potatoes Tapenade

2 large Idaho potatoes, peeled and quartered
¼ cup hot milk
2 cloves garlic, with skins
1 tablespoon anchovy paste, or mashed anchovies
¼ cup olive oil
¼ cup pitted black or green olives
Black pepper
Squeeze of lemon juice

In a medium saucepan, boil the potatoes in salted water until fork-tender and put them through a potato ricer or food mill. Beat in the hot milk.

While the potatoes are cooking, dry-roast the garlic in a skillet until the skins turn spotty black. Remove the skins and put the garlic in a blender with the anchovy paste, olive oil, olives, pepper, and lemon juice, and purée.

Whip the olive-anchovy purée into the riced potatoes and serve hot.

Braised Onions and Lemons

1 lemon
1 large sweet onion, such as Vidalia
2 tablespoons butter or olive oil
⅓ cup dry vermouth
⅛ teaspoon each of ground cinnamon and black pepper

Slice lemon, skin on, as thinly as possible. Remove any seeds.

Peel and slice onion as thinly as possible.

Put lemon and onion in a medium skillet with the remaining ingredients, cover pan, and simmer for 8 to 10 minutes.

◆ This is a sharp palate perker to accompany roast duck, goose, or pork.

◆ If you prefer a sweet-sour taste, simply add a tablespoon of honey to the skillet with the other ingredients.

Lentil-Plantain-Pineapple Ragout

2 cups chicken stock
1 carrot, diced
1 stalk celery, diced
1 medium onion, diced
1 chipotle or other dried chili
2 tomatoes
Salt and black pepper
1 cup lentils
1 slice fresh pineapple, cubed
½ ripe plantain, peeled and sliced

In a large covered pot, simmer the chicken stock, carrot, celery, and half the diced onion for 10 minutes.

In a heavy cast-iron skillet, toast the dried chili (no more than a minute per side), remove stem and seeds, shred the flesh and add to the broth. Pan-roast the whole tomatoes in the same skillet and when their skins are charred, mash them into the stock and mix well. Taste for seasoning and add salt and pepper as wanted.

Add the lentils and simmer, covered, for 15 to 20 minutes, until tender. Add the pineapple and plantain and simmer, covered, 5 minutes more.

Grains, Lentils, and Beans

Chicken Liver Barley
Gorgonzola Risotto
Green Rice
Yogurt Rice
Nutted Wild Rice
Spiced Coconut and Corn Rice
Red Lentils
Yellow Lentil Soup/Stew
Tofu-Miso Stir-Fry
Salsa Grits
Hominy and Shrimp Stew
Black Bean and Hominy Soup

Chicken Liver Barley

1 small onion, chopped
6 tablespoons butter
1 cup pearl barley
2 cups chicken stock, boiling
Salt and black pepper
½ pound chicken livers
½ pound white mushrooms, sliced

In a large skillet, sauté the onion in half the butter until it is golden. Add the barley and sauté until the grains whiten, about 5 minutes. Add the chicken stock and seasonings, cover the pan tightly, and cook over very low heat for 15 minutes.

Melt the remaining butter in a separate skillet and sauté the chicken livers over high heat until they are browned but still pink inside. Remove the livers and chop them coarsely. Brown the mushrooms quickly in the same pan. Add the mushrooms and livers to the barley, stir well with a fork, and cook, covered, until the barley is tender, 10 to 20 minutes more.

◆ Serve with grilled tomatoes. End with pink grapefruit, doused with Port or Marsala, and broiled.

◆ Use the same major ingredients with kasha (buckwheat groats) rather than barley. Toast the kasha in an ungreased skillet; then add a beaten egg and stir rapidly until each grain is separate. In a separate skillet, brown the onion and then the mushrooms and livers and add to the kasha, along with the stock and seasonings. Cover tightly and steam for 30 to 40 minutes, or until the grains are *al dente*.

◆ A soft, rich red will mix well with the liver, especially St. Emilion or California Merlot. Chianti Classico or Lungarotti's Rubesco would be attractive alternatives from Italy.

Gorgonzola Risotto

3 to 4 cups chicken stock
1 tablespoon each of butter and oil
½ small onion, minced
¾ cup Arborio rice
Salt and white pepper
½ cup white wine
2 ounces Gorgonzola cheese, crumbled
2 tablespoons grated Parmesan cheese
2 tablespoons walnuts, chopped
1 tablespoon half-and-half
1 tablespoon chopped fresh Italian parsley for garnish

Bring chicken stock to the simmer in a small saucepan and keep covered.

Heat butter and oil in a large, heavy saucepan and sauté onion for 1 or 2 minutes, to soften. Add rice and stir to coat each grain. Add seasonings and wine and cook slowly until absorbed. Add stock, ½ cup at a time, stirring well each time until liquid is nearly absorbed. When grains are plump and tender but still *al dente* (about 18 to 20 minutes), you don't need more liquid.

Stir in Gorgonzola, Parmesan, walnuts, and half-and-half and mix well, adding a little more stock if desired to make it creamy. Garnish with parsley. Serve immediately.

◆ Serve as a starter or a main dish accompanied by Sautéed Escarole or Wok-Grilled Fennel.

◆ Another classic risotto is based on a mixture of 4 cheeses: Gorgonzola, Fontina, Taleggio, and Parmesan. But almost any cheese, singly or in combination, is delicious. Consider Gruyère, fresh mozzarella, ricotta, mascarpone, goat cheese—you can't go wrong.

◆ Try this dish with a medium-bodied Barolo or Barbaresco.

Green Rice

1 cup basmati rice

SAUCE:
1 tablespoon olive oil
1 tablespoon plain yogurt
2 tablespoons each of chopped fresh parsley and cilantro
1 clove garlic, minced
1 teaspoon fresh lemon juice
½ teaspoon salt
½ teaspoon ground cumin
Black and cayenne peppers

In a large saucepan, bring 2 to 3 quarts of water (with a tablespoon of salt) to a boil. Rinse rice in a strainer under cold water. Add rice to the boiling water and boil briskly about 7 to 8 minutes until tender (taste a few grains after 6 minutes). Drain rice immediately.

Make sauce by putting ingredients into a blender and puréeing. Toss rice with sauce.

◆ Serve as a companion to fish or shellfish in general, and to Chinese Shrimp-in-the-Shell in particular.

◆ Rice is also complemented by other sorts of herbs, such as fresh mint leaves, basil, fennel, arugula. To turn the rice above into a one-dish meal, add some sautéed and chopped shrimp or small clams.

Yogurt Rice

½ cup long-grain rice
1 small fresh chili pepper, minced
2 or 3 slices gingerroot, peeled and minced
½ teaspoon cardamom seeds, crushed
⅛ teaspoon cumin seeds
½ clove garlic, minced
1 tablespoon vegetable oil
½ cup plain yogurt
Salt and black pepper
1 tablespoon chopped fresh cilantro

Wash the rice in a strainer under cold running water until the water runs clear. Bring 2 quarts of salted water to a boil, add the rice, and boil rapidly for 10 to 12 minutes, or until the rice is tender and softer than *al dente.*

Meanwhile, heat the hot pepper, ginger, cardamom, cumin, and garlic in the oil for 2 to 3 minutes and beat into the yogurt. Season with salt and pepper to taste. When the rice is done, drain it well and toss it with the yogurt. Garnish with the cilantro. Serve at any temperature.

Nutted Wild Rice

½ cup wild rice
¾ cup boiling water
2 tablespoons butter
Salt and black pepper
⅓ cup toasted pine nuts

Wash the rice in a sieve under cold running water until the water runs clear, about 2 minutes. Drain and put the rice with the boiling water and 1 teaspoon of the butter into the top of a double boiler. Add salt and pepper to taste, cover, and steam over boiling water for 45 to 55 minutes. Mix with the remaining butter and the pine nuts.

◆ Wild rice is excellent cold, as a salad. If you intend to serve it cold, substitute walnut or olive oil for the butter.

Spiced Coconut and Corn Rice

1 teaspoon sesame seeds
½ teaspoon cumin seeds
½ teaspoon coriander seeds
¼ cup peanuts
1 serrano or other fresh hot chili pepper, seeded and minced
1 tablespoon vegetable oil
2 cups unsweetened coconut milk
¼ cup shredded unsweetened coconut
Salt and black pepper
1 tablespoon butter
1 cup fresh corn kernels
3 cups boiled white rice

Toast the seeds, nuts, and chili lightly in the vegetable oil in a small skillet. Scrape the mixture into a blender and add the coconut milk, shredded coconut, and seasonings. Process until blended but still crunchy.

Heat the butter in the skillet and sauté the corn kernels 2 or 3 minutes to heat them.

Pour the coconut sauce over the cooked rice and top with the corn kernels.

Red Lentils

1 cup red lentils
3 cups chicken stock
½ teaspoon turmeric
3 tablespoons vegetable oil
1 small onion, chopped
2 cloves garlic, minced
1 teaspoon whole cumin seeds
½ teaspoon ground coriander
1 small tomato, seeded and chopped
Salt and cayenne pepper

Pick over lentils to remove any foreign matter and rinse well in a strainer under cold running water. Put lentils in a medium saucepan and cover with chicken stock. Add turmeric and bring to a simmer. Cover partially and simmer until soft, 10 to 15 minutes.

Heat oil in a small skillet, add onion, garlic, cumin, and coriander and sauté 4 to 5 minutes, or until onions are softened. Add tomato and turn mixture into lentils, mixing well. Taste for seasoning. Serve at room temperature.

◆ For a vegetarian meal, accompany the lentils with Yogurt Eggs or Onion-Cheese Soufflé.

◆ Lentils combine nicely with rice. Use the same seasonings, but add ½ cup cooked rice to the cooked lentils.

Yellow Lentil Soup/Stew

1 onion
2 carrots
2 stalks celery
2 tablespoons olive oil
1 clove garlic, minced
¼ teaspoon ground cumin
1 cup yellow lentils
3 cups chicken stock
Large pinch of saffron
Salt and black pepper
2 tablespoons rice
1 tablespoon fresh lemon juice, or to taste

Dice the onions, carrots, and celery. In a large skillet, add oil and sauté vegetables, garlic, and cumin about 5 minutes. Add the lentils, stock, saffron, seasonings, and rice. Bring to the simmer, cover, and cook for 15 minutes. Remove from heat and add lemon juice to taste.

Tofu-Miso Stir-Fry

1 tablespoon miso
½ teaspoon soy sauce
1 tablespoon sherry
3 tablespoons peanut oil
½ pound mushrooms, quartered
2 tablespoons sesame oil
6 green onions with tops, chopped
2 cloves garlic, minced
1 small fresh red or green chili pepper, seeded and minced
¼ teaspoon ground Szechuan pepper
1 square firm tofu, cubed

Soften miso in soy sauce and sherry and set aside.

Place a wok over high heat, add peanut oil, then mushrooms, and sauté quickly to brown them. Remove mushrooms and set aside.

Add sesame oil to the wok, then onions, garlic, chili, and Szechuan pepper and sauté 2 or 3 minutes.

Add softened miso and tofu and toss gently with the other ingredients. Serve hot or at room temperature.

◆ Serve with Red Lentils or Kale and Red Pepper Sauté.

◆ Stir-fry other chopped vegetables such as carrots, celery, turnips, eggplant, or zucchini, before adding tofu and/or fresh bean sprouts.

◆ This dish is perfect for crisp, off-dry wines like Vouvray Sec and German QbA Riesling.

Salsa Grits

3 cups water
1 cup milk
1 teaspoon salt
1 cup quick grits (see Note below)
4 tablespoons butter
1 cup shredded Monterey Jack cheese

SALSA:
2 ripe tomatoes
½ small onion, finely chopped
1 jalapeño or serrano chili
4 sprigs fresh cilantro
Salt and black pepper

Bring the water and milk to boil in a large saucepan. Add the salt and stir in the grits. Lower the heat and simmer until the grits thicken, about 5 minutes. Stir in the butter and cheese.

To make the salsa, broil the tomatoes, turning them to char the skin on all sides. Purée them, skin and all, in a blender. Remove the stem, seeds, and veins of the chili and mince the flesh. Chop the cilantro. Mix all ingredients together and taste for seasoning. Make a well in the cooked grits and pour in the salsa.

◆ Good with steamed asparagus or sautéed string beans.

◆ To make fried grits, cook the grits the night before. Spread them in a pan and chill. Cut into ½-inch slices; then dip in beaten egg and fresh bread crumbs mixed with grated Parmesan cheese and fry the slices in butter. Pass the salsa in a bowl.

◆ Choose a dry, easy red with some zest: inexpensive Zinfandel, a Côtes du Ventoux, or Valpolicella.

Note: If you can find old-fashioned stoneground grits, prepare them as quick grits, but increase the cooking time 45 to 60 minutes.

Hominy and Shrimp Stew

2 cups fish stock or clam juice
½ pound shrimp in the shell
1 small onion, diced
1 clove garlic, minced
1 tablespoon butter
1 tablespoon olive oil
1 sweet red pepper, roasted, seeded, and diced
1 jalapeño pepper, roasted, seeded, and diced
1 cup cooked or canned hominy, drained
1 tablespoon fresh lime juice
1 tablespoon fresh cilantro, chopped

Bring the stock to the boil in a small saucepan, add the shrimp, cover, and remove it from the heat. Let sit 5 minutes, then remove the shrimp with a slotted spoon and peel off the shells. Reserve the shrimp, add the shells to the fish stock, cover, and simmer 15 minutes. Remove the shells and save the liquid.

In a medium saucepan, sauté the onion and garlic in the butter and oil until softened, about 5 minutes. Add the sweet and hot peppers and sauté 2 or 3 minutes more. Add the shrimp liquid and the hominy and bring to a boil. Remove from the heat and add the shrimp, lime juice, and cilantro.

◆ A California Sauvignon Blanc will suit the flavors of this dish quite well.

Black Bean and Hominy Stew

1 ham hock, or 1 ham steak with bone (see Note below)
2 carrots, chopped
1 onion, chopped
2 cloves garlic, mashed
1 tablespoon fresh oregano, or 1 teaspoon dried
1 bay leaf
2 cloves allspice
1 cup black beans
1 tablespoon chipotle chili in adobo
1 sweet red pepper, diced
1 cup hominy
Salt and black pepper
Avocado and radish for garnish (optional)

In a large saucepan, cover the ham, carrots, onion, garlic, herbs, and spices with water and simmer until the meat is tender (1½ to 2 hours). Strain the liquid into another pan and when the ham hock is cool, remove meat and skin from the bone and dice it finely.

Add the beans to the liquid with the chipotle chili, cover, and simmer about 1 hour, until the beans are tender. Add the red pepper and hominy and taste for seasoning before adding salt and pepper.

Chop the avocado and slice radishes for garnish.

◆ Try a large-bodied Zinfandel from Napa or Sonoma with this sturdy stew; it should hold up well and complement the strong flavors of the dish. As would one of the many well-made Mouvedres coming out of California.

Note: You won't get the same flavor from a ham steak, but you can reduce the initial cooking time to 20 or 30 minutes.

Pasta and Polenta

Lemon and Red Pepper Pasta
Pasta with Roasted Peanuts
Pasta with Anchovy, Fennel, and Feta
Pasta with Black Beans and Sun-Dried Tomatoes
Pasta with Artichokes and Olives
Pasta with Avocado Cream
Pesto, Pasta, and Potatoes
Penne with Charred Vegetables
Angel's Hair with Caviar
Mustard-Lemon Linguine with Asparagus
Leek and Arugula Fettuccine
Fettuccine with Oysters
Orzo with Pine Nuts and Currants
Sesame-Scallop Noodles
Sweet Lemon Noodles
Orange-Almond Fettuccine
Polenta with Poached Eggs
Buckwheat Polenta with Endives
Couscous Polenta
Polenta with Prosciutto, Figs, and Olives
Polenta Foie Gras

Lemon and Red Pepper Pasta

2 tablespoons butter
1 sweet red pepper
1 lemon
1 cup heavy cream or crème fraîche
Salt and black and cayenne peppers
½ pound fresh fettuccine
Grated Parmesan cheese

In a large saucepan, bring 3 quarts of water (with a tablespoon of salt and a teaspoon of oil) to a boil.

Meanwhile, prepare the sauce. Melt the butter in a large skillet or saucepan. Quarter the pepper and remove the stem and seeds; then dice the flesh and add it to the skillet. Grate the lemon rind into the skillet and add the juice of half the lemon, the cream, and salt and peppers. Keep the sauce warm, but well below a simmer.

Add the pasta to the boiling water, test after 1 or 2 minutes, and keep testing until it is *al dente*. Drain immediately and toss the pasta in the sauce. Serve with a bowl of grated Parmesan cheese.

◆ Serve with a watercress salad and follow with Blackened Figs.

◆ For a different vegetable crunch, add fresh corn kernels and lightly steamed asparagus tips to the same lemon-cream sauce.

◆ Lemon and cream with pasta call for a dry white from Italy: Gavi, Orvieto Secco, or, for something slightly more exotic, a Fiano di Avellino. A very dry Chenin Blanc from California might also work well.

Pasta with Roasted Peanuts

1½ tablespoons olive oil
1 small onion, chopped
1 to 2 cloves garlic, minced
1 tomato, seeded and chopped
2 to 3 slices gingerroot, minced
Black and cayenne peppers
1 tablespoon peanut butter
½ teaspoon soy sauce
½ cup chicken stock
⅓ pound dried pasta (farfalle, penne, macaroni)
⅓ cup roasted peanuts, chopped
3 or 4 sprigs fresh cilantro for garnish

Bring 3 quarts of water (with a tablespoon of salt and a teaspoon of olive oil) to a boil.

Prepare the sauce by heating the oil in a small skillet and sautéing onion and garlic 4 to 5 minutes, until softened. Add tomato, ginger, and black and cayenne peppers. Thin peanut butter with soy sauce and chicken stock and add to mixture in skillet. Bring liquid to a simmer, cover pan, and remove from heat.

Cook pasta in the boiling water, test after 3 or 4 minutes, and cook until *al dente.* Drain and toss pasta with sauce. Garnish with chopped peanuts and cilantro sprigs.

◆ Serve hot or at room temperature with Chinese Cabbage and Pink Grapefruit Slaw, fresh green beans, or a mixed green salad.

◆ Use the same peanut sauce for a stir-fry dish of pork slivers, chunks of chicken, shrimp, or tofu, mixed with bean sprouts and fresh or dried hot chili pepper.

◆ With this dish, try an acidic wine with a touch of sweetness, such as a QbA Riesling from the Mosel, or a light Riesling from Washington State.

Pasta with Anchovy, Fennel, and Feta

1 head fennel
1 tablespoon each *of butter and olive oil*
1 to 2 cloves garlic, minced
2 green onions with tops, chopped
6 to 8 anchovy fillets, plus 1 tablespoon of their oil, or 2 teaspoons anchovy
  paste, plus 1 tablespoon olive oil
Black pepper
⅓ pound spaghettini (or other dried pasta)
⅓ cup crumbled feta cheese

Bring 3 quarts of water (with a tablespoon of salt and a teaspoon of oil) to a boil.

Cut off and discard the root end and stalky tops of the fennel, saving ¼ cup of the ferny leaves, plus a few sprigs for garnish. Trim off any discolored areas on the outside layer of the fennel, then slice the head crosswise. Chop the reserved fennel leaves. In a medium skillet, heat butter and oil and sauté fennel with garlic and onions about 3 to 5 minutes, until somewhat softened. Chop anchovies and add with their oil to fennel. Add black pepper and the chopped fennel leaves.

Cook pasta in the boiling water, test after 3 or 4 minutes, and cook until *al dente.* Drain and toss with fennel mixture and crumbled feta cheese. Garnish with fennel sprigs.

◆ Serve with a light salad and a Plum Mascarpone Tart with Quick Nut Crust.

◆ Instead of anchovies, use chopped freshly brined sardines or smoked mussels. For a subtler effect, simmer a quarter of the fennel in chicken or fish stock to cover, and purée with a tablespoon of feta in a blender. Thin sauce with more stock or cream and add a dash of Pernod.

◆ The salt from the anchovies and feta and the licorice flavors from the fennel reach out for fruity, refreshing white wines such as Vouvray Sec and German Kabinett Riesling from the Rhein.

Pasta with Black Beans and Sun-Dried Tomatoes

4 slices pancetta, or bacon
2 tablespoons olive oil
1 small onion, chopped fine
2 cloves garlic, minced
4 sun-dried tomatoes, diced
1 small fresh red or green chili pepper, seeded and minced
¼ cup white wine
1 cup cooked black beans (or fava, pea beans, cannellini, Great Northern), (reserve bean liquid for possible use)
Salt and black pepper
⅓ pound dried pasta (macaroni, shells, penne)
Grated Parmesan or Pecorino cheese

Bring 3 quarts of water (with a tablespoon of salt and a teaspoon of oil) to a boil.

In a medium skillet, fry pancetta or bacon until crisp, remove, cut in small pieces, and reserve. Pour out all but a teaspoon of fat. Heat the oil with the fat and add onion, garlic, tomatoes, and chili pepper. Sauté 4 or 5 minutes until vegetables are softened, add wine, drained beans, and seasonings, and bring to a simmer. (If sauce is too thick, add some of the bean liquid.) Remove from heat and keep sauce warm until ready to use.

Cook pasta in the boiling water, test after 3 or 4 minutes, and cook until *al dente*. Drain and mix the pasta with beans, add the sauce, and serve with grated cheese.

◆ Serve hot with crusty semolina bread and a mixed green or a fresh fruit salad.

◆ Turn pasta and bean combination into a soup, as in *pasta e fagioli*, by using 3 ounces pasta to 3 cups chicken stock. Mash some of the beans to thicken the liquid and add a couple of seeded and chopped fresh tomatoes.

◆ Sturdy, young red wines like Nebbiolo d'Alba or Côtes du Rhône Villages are perfect companions to hardy bean pasta dishes.

Pasta with Artichokes and Olives

2 large artichokes
1 tablespoon olive oil
Juice of ½ lemon
1 tablespoon butter
½ small onion, chopped
½ cup green olives, Mediterranean style
½ cup heavy cream
Salt and black pepper
½ pound fresh tagliatelle
Grated Parmesan cheese

Leave the full stems on artichokes but tear off all the fibrous outer leaves and trim off the base of the leaves all around to get to the outside of the heart. Cut off and discard the top half of the artichokes. Cut the bottom half into quarters or eighths and carve out the chokes (small hairs on top of the heart). In a medium saucepan, simmer artichokes in ⅔ cup water with oil and lemon juice, covered, for about 10 minutes, or until artichokes are tender.

Remove artichokes, add butter and onion, and simmer 4 or 5 minutes, or until onions are softened. Pit the green olives and add olives and artichokes to the onions. Add cream, seasonings, and bring to a simmer. Keep sauce warm until ready to use.

Bring 3 quarts of water (with a tablespoon of salt and a teaspoon of oil) to a boil. Add pasta, test after 1 minute, and drain the moment it reaches *al dente.* Toss with the sauce and serve with Parmesan cheese and an extra sprinkling of black pepper.

◆ Serve as a main dish after Wok-Smoked Trout or Roasted Oysters with Curry Butter.

◆ If you don't have time to prepare fresh artichokes, buy artichoke hearts preserved in oil or cook frozen artichoke hearts and then sauté them in oil with the onion. Increase flavor with fresh herbs, such as mint, oregano, or chopped parsley.

◆ Artichokes can pose problems for some wines—turning them dull and insipid—but crisp, fruity Italian wines, like Sauvignon Blancs and Pinot Grigios from Friuli, do just fine.

Pasta with Avocado Cream

¼ onion, diced
1 to 2 jalapeño peppers, seeded and chopped
2 tablespoons olive oil
½ ripe avocado, chunked
Salt and black pepper
2 tablespoons fresh lime juice
2 tablespoons fresh cilantro
1 cup chicken stock
½ pound fresh fettucine, or similar pasta
Thin slices of Parmesan cheese

Bring 3 quarts of water (with a tablespoon of salt and a teaspoon of oil) to a boil.

In a medium skillet, sauté the onion and jalapeño in the oil until softened. Scrape them into a blender and add the remaining ingredients except for the pasta and Parmesan cheese. Purée until smooth. Return the sauce to the sauté pan and bring just to a simmer.

Add the pasta to the boiling water, test after 1 or 2 minutes, and keep testing until it is *al dente*. Drain well.

Toss the pasta with the green sauce and top with thin slices of good Parmesan cheese.

◆ You want a simple, direct wine—Chablis would not be a shabby mate for this subtle dish. Or, to keep it Italian and less edgy, try a good white from Orvieto, served very cold.

Pesto, Pasta, and Potatoes

PESTO SAUCE:
1 cup fresh basil leaves, packed
¼ cup parsley sprigs
¼ cup olive oil
1 to 2 cloves garlic
Pinch of salt
¼ cup pine nuts or walnuts
⅓ cup grated Parmesan cheese (buy 2 ounces for the entire recipe)

PASTA AND POTATOES:
4 small red new potatoes
¼ pound string beans
3 green onions with tops, minced
Salt and black pepper
½ pound dried pasta (penne, fusilli, farfalle, orecchiette)
½ cup grated Parmesan cheese

Make the pesto by puréeing all the sauce ingredients in a blender or processor. If the sauce is too thick to handle, add a tablespoon of soft butter or a little more oil.

In a small saucepan, boil the potatoes in their skins until fork-tender, about 10 minutes. Drain and cool; then slice thin.

Trim the beans and boil them in a small saucepan until they are no longer "raw" but are still crisp, about 5 to 8 minutes. Drain. In a large bowl, mix the onions with the beans and potatoes. Season lightly with salt and pepper.

Boil the pasta in 3 quarts of water (with a tablespoon of salt and a teaspoon of oil) until *al dente*. Drain and toss the pasta, potatoes, beans, and onions with the pesto and serve with a bowl of the Parmesan.

◆ Serve with an escarole salad. Finish with a platter of cheese.

◆ To make pesto burgers, mix half the pesto with a pound of

ground chuck or ground lamb. Add salt and pepper to taste and shape into two large patties. Sauté the patties in a tablespoon *each* of butter and oil to make the patties crusty on the outside but rare within.

◆ A fairly sweet California Riesling will cut the garlic. If you lean toward red, look for a substantial Nebbiolo from northern Italy, such as Ghemme, Spanna, or Gattinara. Even Barolo would be traditionally appropriate.

Penne with Charred Vegetables

1 tablespoon olive oil
1 small onion
½ sweet red pepper
½ small (or 1 Japanese) eggplant
½ small zucchini
2 cloves garlic
⅓ pound penne, or other dried pasta
Salt and black pepper

Bring 3 quarts of water (with a tablespoon of salt and a teaspoon of oil) to a boil.

Cut onions into eighths. Cut halved red pepper into ½-inch strips. Cut halved eggplant and zucchini lengthwise into slices ¼ inch thick. Peel and slice the garlic.

Heat a wok or heavy skillet until very hot. Add the oil, then onion and red pepper. Turn vegetables to char on all sides, then remove to a warm platter. Add eggplant, zucchini, and garlic. Char vegetables as quickly as possible, turning to brown on both sides, then add to onion and peppers.

Cook pasta in boiling water, test after 3 or 4 minutes, and cook until *al dente*. Drain and mix with vegetables, seasoning to taste.

◆ This is a hearty meal in itself. Follow with a light dessert such as Gingered Figs.

◆ Anything charred this way is going to complement the blandness of pasta, so try different kinds of vegetables or small fish fillets, shrimp, or very thin strips of beef. Or, if you want more of a sauce, purée some of the charred vegetables for a nice smoky taste.

◆ Light, fruity red wines, like Beaujolais and Dolcetta d'Alba, cozy right up to the blackened veggies in this dish.

Angel's Hair with Caviar

⅓ pound angel's hair pasta (capellini)
½ cup fish stock or clam juice
3 tablespoons butter
1 cup crème fraîche or sour cream
¼ cup chopped chives
Black pepper
Grated rind of 1 lemon
2 ounces sturgeon or golden whitefish caviar

Bring 3 quarts of water (with a tablespoon of salt and a teaspoon of oil) to a boil. Add the pasta, stir well, and cook rapidly. Test after 1 or 2 minutes by forking out a strand and nibbling the end of it. Keep testing until it has the right chewy tenderness—*al dente*—on your teeth.

Meanwhile, in a skillet or saucepan large enough to toss the pasta, bring the stock to a boil and melt the butter in it. Remove from the heat, add the cream and chives, and keep the sauce warm.

Drain the pasta the moment it is done and toss it thoroughly in the sauce. Grind black pepper over the top and sprinkle with the lemon rind and caviar.

◆ Serve with a stir-fry of snow peas and slivered sweet red peppers. End with Fresh Fruit Macedonia.

◆ Angel's hair with mascarpone cheese: Put ½ cup mascarpone in a blender with 3 tablespoons of melted butter and 1 to 2 tablespoons Gorgonzola cheese. Blend with 1½ cups of heavy cream. Season to taste and toss with the cooked pasta. Thin the sauce, if needed, with dry vermouth.

◆ Caviar always suggests a sparkling wine, though real Champagne isn't absolutely necessary: a sparkling white from the Loire or California is just as appropriate. A bottle of Codorniu from Spain would be another, even less expensive, possibility. If you prefer something without effervescence, try the full-flavored Vernacchia from Italy.

Mustard–Lemon Linguine with Asparagus

4 to 6 spears asparagus
2 tablespoons butter
1 tablespoon olive oil
1 to 1½ tablespoons Dijon mustard
1 cup heavy cream
Rind and juice of ½ lemon
Salt and black pepper
⅓ pound dried linguine
Grated Parmesan cheese

Bring 3 quarts of water (with a tablespoon of salt and a teaspoon of oil) to a boil.

Bring about 1 cup of salted water to a boil in a skillet just large enough to hold the asparagus spears. Simmer asparagus 4 to 6 minutes (depending on size), until just fork-tender but still crisp. Remove spears but save liquid in a bowl.

Make sauce by heating butter and oil in a small saucepan. Beat in mustard and cream, and simmer for 3 or 4 minutes. Add lemon rind, juice, and seasonings, and keep warm while cooking the pasta.

Cook linguine in the boiling water, test after 3 or 4 minutes, and cook until *al dente*. Drain and toss pasta with sauce and asparagus. If sauce is too thick, add a little asparagus juice. Sprinkle with Parmesan cheese.

◆ Serve with Sautéed Escarole and Chili Oranges.

◆ For a creamy sauce without cream, roast a dozen garlic cloves in their skins in the butter and oil, enclosed in foil, at 350°F. for about 10 minutes (roasted garlic loses its edge and has a rich, nutty taste). Remove garlic and press flesh from the skins into the butter and oil. Put in a blender with the mustard, lemon, and ¼ cup white wine (or asparagus juice) and blend until smooth.

◆ Look for a light, fairly neutral white wine like an Italian Chardonnay or a white Bordeaux from the region of Entre-deux-Mers.

Leek and Arugula Fettuccine

1 bunch arugula
2 tablespoons butter
2 sprigs fresh mint
2 to 3 tablespoons dry vermouth
Salt and black pepper
2 leeks
2 tablespoons olive oil
½ pound fettuccine, or other fresh noodles

Bring 3 quarts of water (with a tablespoon of salt and a teaspoon of oil) to a boil.

Meanwhile, cut the stems from the arugula and wash the leaves well. Melt the butter in a large skillet and sauté the leaves for 2 or 3 minutes. Put the arugula, mint, vermouth, and salt and pepper in the blender and purée until smooth. Taste for seasoning.

Cut off the roots and tops of the leeks and wash the leeks well. Cut them in half lengthwise and shred finely. Sauté the leeks in the oil until tender but not browned. Add the arugula purée to the leeks and keep the sauce warm.

Add the pasta to the boiling water, test after 1 or 2 minutes, and keep testing until it is *al dente*. Drain immediately and toss the pasta in the sauce.

◆ Finish with a coffee *granita* or a lemon sorbet.

◆ For pasta with puréed peas and mint, quickly sauté a handful of sugar-snap peas (or snow peas) in 3 tablespoons of butter in a covered skillet. Purée them in a processor with a sprig or two of mint, salt, pepper, and nutmeg; then thin the purée with hot cream and toss with the pasta and some grated Parmesan cheese.

◆ If you prefer white, look for Pinot Grigio, dry Orvieto, or Tunina. For red, either Chianti Classico, Rubesco, or Ghemme would provide the right combination of full flavor and medium body.

Fettuccine with Oysters

1 cup shucked oysters, plus their liquid
3 tablespoons butter
1 teaspoon fresh thyme, or ¼ teaspoon dried thyme
Salt and black pepper
¾ cup crème fraîche or heavy cream
1 teaspoon fresh lemon juice
½ pound fresh fettuccine
Grated Parmesan cheese
Fresh thyme sprigs for garnish

Bring 3 quarts of water (with a tablespoon of salt and a teaspoon of oil) to a boil.

Drain oysters and reserve ¼ cup of their liquid. Heat butter in a large skillet and sauté oysters gently over medium-low heat, with thyme and seasonings, for 1 or 2 minutes. Add oyster liquid, remove from heat, and stir in the crème fraîche. (If using heavy cream, remove oysters, add oyster liquid and cream to the pan, and reduce until just thickened.) Add lemon juice to taste and keep sauce warm (but not over direct heat) while cooking the pasta.

Cook pasta in boiling water, test after 1 minute, and drain the moment it reaches *al dente*. Immediately toss pasta with sauce and sprinkle with cheese and a few sprigs of fresh thyme.

◆ Serve as a one-dish meal and, for an all-white meal, finish with Pernod Pears.

◆ The same sauce works well with other seafood, such as tiny clams, scallops, crab, or lobster. For a ritzy occasion, garnish the sauce with fresh sturgeon, golden whitefish, or salmon caviar.

◆ Try a Friulian Pinot Bianco, Alsatian Pinot Blanc, or crisp Oregon Chardonnay.

Orzo with Pine Nuts and Currants

3 cups chicken stock
½ cup dried currants
1 cup orzo
1 tablespoon olive oil
4 green onions with tops, chopped
½ cup pine nuts
Salt and black pepper

In a large saucepan, bring stock to the boil, add currants and orzo, lower heat, and let liquid simmer for 8 to 10 minutes, or until liquid is largely absorbed and the pasta is *al dente*.

Meanwhile, heat oil in a small skillet and sauté onions and pine nuts for 3 or 4 minutes until golden. Add to the orzo, with seasonings, when the pasta is done.

◆ Serve as an accompaniment to a roast lamb, chicken, or rabbit, or to a grilled fish.

◆ Orzo in shape and texture is somewhat like rice. Try mixing it with chopped wild mushrooms, such as chanterelles, dried cherries, or apricots that have been soaked in Madeira.

Sesame–Scallop Noodles

½ pound egg noodles (fresh is best)
1 tablespoon sesame oil
½ pound scallops
2 tablespoons toasted sesame seeds
2 green onions with tops, finely chopped
3 tablespoons tahini or fresh peanut butter
¼ cup brewed tea
1 tablespoon soy sauce
1 teaspoon sugar
1 teaspoon wine vinegar
½ clove garlic, minced
Minced fresh chili pepper, red pepper flakes, or cayenne pepper

Boil the fresh noodles in 3 quarts of water (with a tablespoon of salt and a teaspoon of oil) for about 2 minutes or until *al dente*. Drain and rinse with cold water. Drain again and mix in a bowl with 1 teaspoon of the sesame oil.

If using sea scallops, cut them into quarters. Add the remaining sesame oil to a hot wok or skillet and sauté the scallops, turning, about 1 minute. Add to the noodles with the sesame seeds and green onions.

Put the remaining ingredients in a blender to make a sauce. Thin or thicken as desired with more tea or tahini. Adjust the spiciness to your taste. Toss the noodle mixture in the sauce. Serve at room temperature.

◆ Good with a crunchy green vegetable like snow peas or broccoli.

◆ For a very different effect, toss the hot noodles and scallops with ½ cup toasted poppy seeds puréed in a blender with 4 tablespoons of melted butter. Season with salt and pepper to taste and serve at once.

◆ The spiciness here is best matched by a semi-sweet white: try a Chenin Blanc from California or a Vouvray Demi-Sec.

Sweet Lemon Noodles (Dessert Pasta)

4 tablespoons butter
½ pound fresh ricotta cheese
½ cup mascarpone
2 to 3 tablespoons sugar
Rind and juice of 1 lemon
½ pound fresh fettuccine, or other egg noodles

Bring 3 quarts of water (with a tablespoon of salt and a teaspoon of oil) to a boil.

Melt butter in a medium saucepan. Remove from heat and blend in ricotta and mascarpone until smooth. Add sugar, lemon rind, and juice. Taste and add more sugar if desired.

Cook pasta in boiling water, taste after 1 minute, and drain the moment the pasta is *al dente*. Toss pasta with the sauce.

◆ Serve as a dessert after a light meal, such as Steamed Clams with Vegetables.

◆ For a savory/unsweetened pasta, simply eliminate sugar and make a lemon-flavored cheese sauce. Or, for another form of dessert using ricotta and mascarpone, fill a prebaked pastry crust with the mixture and sprinkle the top with toasted almonds or candied lemon slices.

◆ Accompany this simple but delicious preparation with an unusual dessert wine, such as a sharp, lemony Malvasia from Sicily.

Orange–Almond Fettuccine (Dessert Pasta)

4 tablespoons butter
Rind and juice of 2 oranges
⅓ cup sugar
½ teaspoon ground cinnamon
¼ teaspoon black pepper
½ pound fresh fettuccine
½ cup toasted almonds, chopped
⅓ cup grated Parmesan cheese

Bring 3 quarts of water (with a tablespoon of salt and a teaspoon of oil) to a boil.

Melt butter in a medium saucepan. Reserve orange rind but add just ¾ cup of orange juice to butter. Add sugar and turn heat to high until liquid begins to turn amber. Remove from heat, add rind, cinnamon, and pepper.

Cook pasta in the boiling water, test after 1 minute, and drain the moment the pasta is *al dente*. Toss with sauce and sprinkle it with nuts and cheese.

◆ Serve after a meal of Pan-Grilled Portobello Mushrooms or Turkey Scallopini.

◆ For a molded and baked pasta dessert, use but ¼ cup orange juice beaten with 2 eggs and ½ pound fresh ricotta or farmer's cheese. Add the other ingredients as above. Sprinkle a buttered 1-quart mold with Parmesan cheese and alternate layers of cooked fettuccine with cheese mixture. Bake at 375°F. for 20 to 30 minutes until top is browned. Unmold and serve.

◆ For an interesting twist, serve this dessert with a sweet white, such as nutty Tuscan Vin Santo.

Polenta with Poached Eggs

2 slices Italian pancetta, or Canadian bacon
2 tablespoons butter
1 cup cooked polenta, well-chilled
4 eggs, poached and kept warm
Salt and black pepper
½ cup grated Parmesan cheese

Sauté the pancetta in 1 tablespoon of the butter in a large, heavy skillet until slightly browned. Remove and set aside. Cut the polenta in two 4- to 5-inch squares, about an inch thick. Reheat the skillet and brown the polenta well on both sides.

Top each polenta square with a piece of pancetta and a pair of poached eggs. Season the eggs, cover them with Parmesan cheese, and dot with the remaining tablespoon of butter. Run the skillet under a broiler for 2 or 3 minutes to brown the cheese.

◆ If you want to go for broke, substitute hollandaise sauce for the cheese and turn the dish into Eggs Benedict, or substitute a good tomato salsa and turn it into a version of Huevos Rancheros.

Buckwheat Polenta with Endives

½ cup polenta taragna, or mix half cornmeal and half buckwheat groats
2 cups hot chicken stock
2 tablespoons butter
2 Belgian endives, split lengthwise
1 tablespoon olive oil
1 clove garlic, minced
Salt and black pepper
½ cup grated Parmesan cheese

Soften the polenta in the top of a double boiler with ¼ cup cold water. Gradually stir in the hot stock and mix until smooth. Cover the top and place it over the bottom pan, filled with an inch or two of boiling water. Steam for 40 to 50 minutes. Add the butter, and salt it if needed. Keep warm.

While the polenta cooks, marinate the endive in the oil, garlic, and seasonings. When the polenta is done, heat a large, heavy skillet, place the endive cut-side down in the skillet, with its marinade, and brown the endive well on both sides. Serve the endive and its juices on top of the polenta and sprinkle with Parmesan.

Couscous Polenta

1 tablespoon butter
1 tablespoon olive oil
½ small onion, diced
½ cup whole-grain polenta
2 cups hot chicken stock
Salt and black and cayenne peppers

TOPPING:
½ small fennel bulb, slivered
4 green onions, white part slivered
1 tablespoon olive oil
½ cup blanched slivered almonds
¼ cup raisins
1 tablespoon zatar, or mix equal parts thyme and sesame seeds

Heat the butter and oil in the top of a double boiler, sauté the onion 3 or 4 minutes, then add the polenta and toast it, stirring constantly until golden brown. Add the chicken stock gradually and season to taste. Cover the top and place it over the bottom pan, filled with an inch or two of boiling water. Steam until the polenta has thickened.

Meanwhile, in a small hot skillet sauté the fennel and onions in the olive oil until browned. Lower the heat to moderate and add the almonds, raisins, and zatar. Sauté 2 to 3 minutes, until the almonds are toasted.

Scoop the cooked polenta onto a platter and cover it with the topping.

Polenta with Prosciutto, Figs, and Olives

½ cup whole-grain polenta
2 cups hot chicken stock
Salt and black pepper
1 tablespoon olive oil
¼ pound prosciutto, shredded
6 fresh figs, quartered
12 Mediterranean small green olives

Make the polenta 2 or 3 hours ahead of time in order to mold, chill, and slice it for pan-grilling. Put the polenta in the top of a double boiler, add ¼ cup cold water, then stir in the hot stock gradually, along with seasoning, and mix until smooth. Cover the top, place it over the bottom of the pan, filled with an inch or two of boiling water, and steam 30 to 40 minutes. When the polenta is thick, scrape it into a small round or square mold, or wrap it in a rectangle of foil, and chill it in the refrigerator. When cold enough to slice it, make 4 slices 1-inch thick.

Heat the oil in a large heavy skillet until very hot and pan-grill the polenta slices on both sides until well browned. Remove them to a warm platter. In the same skillet, sauté the shredded prosciutto just long enough to heat it and pile it over the slices. Quickly pan-grill the quartered figs with the olives and place them on the prosciutto.

◆ Serve one of the fine Oregon Pinot Noirs with this rustic Italian dish—look for the wines of Sokol Blosser and Ponzi. Or go with the superb Saintsbury Pinot Noir Garnet that is lightly redolent of berries, which Parker compares to a good Côte de Beaune.

Polenta Foie Gras

½ cup whole-grain polenta
2 cups hot chicken stock
Salt and black pepper
⅓ cup foie gras pâté
⅓ cup toasted hazelnuts, chopped

Put the polenta in the top of a double boiler and moisten it with ¼ cup cold water. Add the hot stock gradually and stir until smooth. Add the seasoning. Cover the top and place it over the bottom of the pan, filled with an inch or two of boiling water. Steam until the polenta is thick, 30 to 40 minutes, then stir in the foie gras and mix until smooth. Garnish the top with toasted hazelnuts.

◆ If you're feeling flush and reckless, garnish this velvety dish with slivers of black or shavings of white truffle.

Shellfish

Black Pepper Shrimp
Corn and Shrimp Brûlée
Charred Shrimp Poblano
Brandied Clam Stew
Steamed Clams with Vegetables
Clam and Sausage Chowder
Scallops with Hazelnuts
Wok-Smoked Scallops with Green Sauce
Scallops in Orange Butter
Oyster Cream Stew
Coconut Shellfish Curry
Mussels in Hot Potato Salad
Lobster Tarragon
Lobster with Avocado and Tequila
Soft-Shell Crabs in Black Butter
Salsa Squid

Black Pepper Shrimp

1½ pounds large raw shrimp in the shell
¼ pound butter
2 tablespoons freshly ground black pepper
2 cloves garlic, minced

Rinse and drain the shrimp and put them in a baking dish in a single layer. Cut the butter into pieces and put them on top of the shrimp. Sprinkle the pepper and garlic over the whole. Bake at 350°F. for 30 minutes, turning the shrimp once or twice to coat the shells with the butter.

◆ Serve the shrimp with French or Italian bread (and a couple of hot washcloths), because you will peel the shrimp as you go and sop up the butter with hunks of bread.

Accompany the shrimp with a salad you can also eat with your fingers: asparagus spears or endive and arugula. End with Sautéed Peaches and Cream.

◆ Broil the shrimp (or other shellfish) by dipping them into a mixture of 4 tablespoons *each* of melted butter and olive oil. Then roll each piece in a mixture of dried herbs, such as thyme, rosemary, oregano, marjoram, summer savory, or basil. Broil quickly for 3 to 5 minutes, turning the shrimp once. Heat the remaining butter and oil and use as a dipping sauce.

◆ This is a perfect occasion for a good Premier Cru Chablis or Sancerre from France. California Sauvignon Blanc could be an alternative, or, for a change, try a fino sherry.

Corn and Shrimp Brûlée

3 ears sweet corn (about 2 cups kernels)
½ pound shrimp, peeled
2 tablespoons butter, melted
1 jalapeño pepper, minced
4 eggs, beaten
1 cup heavy cream
Salt and black and cayenne peppers
2 to 3 tablespoons brown sugar

Cut the kernels from the ears of corn. With the back of your knife, scrape the cobs to get all the corns "milk."

If the shrimp are large, cut them in half or into quarters. Mix the corn and shrimp with the butter, jalapeño pepper, eggs, cream, and salt and peppers. Bake in a buttered 8-inch pie pan (set in a pan of boiling water) at 300°F. for 30 to 40 minutes, or until the custard is almost set. Sprinkle the top with the brown sugar and run the dish under a hot broiler to brown and form a glaze, watching carefully so the sugar doesn't burn.

◆ Serve with sliced tomatoes and basil. Finish with boysenberry ice and oatmeal cookies.

◆ Make a corn and shrimp souffléd pudding from the same ingredients except the sugar. Scald the cream. Separate 4 eggs. Beat the yolks until foamy; then gradually beat in the cream, corn, shrimp, butter, jalapeño, and seasonings. Beat the egg whites until stiff but not dry and fold into the mixture. Bake in a 6-cup buttered straight-sided baking dish at 375°F. for 40 to 50 minutes.

◆ Something with a hint of sweetness would take the edge off the hot pepper here: California Chenin Blanc, Orvieto Abboccato, or a Vouvray Demi-Sec.

Charred Shrimp Poblano

1 pound medium or large shrimp in their shells
1 cup white wine, or water
2 tomatoes
2 cloves garlic, peeled
1 chili poblano (see Note that follows) or 2 jalapeños
1 small onion, cut into eighths
2 tablespoons olive oil
3 tablespoons chopped fresh cilantro
Salt

Peel and devein shrimp. Set the shrimp aside and put their shells in a small saucepan with a wine. Bring liquid to a boil, cover, and cook 15 minutes. Remove shells and boil liquid down to ¼ cup.

Put tomatoes, garlic, chili, and onion in a small oiled baking pan and drizzle 1 tablespoon of olive oil over the vegetables. Roast uncovered at 400°F. for about 30 minutes, until onion is soft. When the chili is cool enough to handle, remove and discard the stem, cut chili in half and remove seeds. Process chili, tomatoes, garlic, and onion in a blender. Add cilantro, salt, and reserved shrimp liquid, and purée until smooth.

Heat a wok or large cast-iron skillet over high heat. Put in remaining tablespoon of oil and when it begins to smoke, add shrimp, turning to char on all sides. Put sauce on a platter and place shrimp on top.

◆ Serve as a first course for Fresh Corn Tamale Pie or as a main dish with Roast Potato Chips or Honeyed Golden Peppers.

◆ If you want to char the shrimp in their shells (as in Chinese Shrimp-in-the-Shell), serve the sauce as a dipping sauce. Or serve with the fresh salsa used in Salsa Squid.

◆ Crisp, fresh fino sherry, served ice-cold, is a terrific accompaniment to this tapas-like preparation.

Note: If you use a dried poblano (called chili ancho), rinse it, remove stem and seeds, then toast for a minute or two in a hot skillet, and add to the shrimp shells and wine. Instead of discarding it with the shells, put chili in the blender to purée with the other blender ingredients.

Brandied Clam Stew

2 dozen hard-shelled clams
½ cup dry white wine
4 tablespoons butter
1 large onion, finely chopped
1 clove garlic, minced
1 Idaho baking potato, peeled and diced
1 pint half-and-half
Black pepper, lemon juice, Worcestershire and Tabasco sauces
¼ cup Cognac

Scrub the clams under cold running water to get rid of any sand. Put them into a large covered pot with the wine and steam over low heat until the shells open, 7 to 10 minutes. Strain the clam liquid in a strainer lined with cheesecloth or folded paper towels. Remove the clams from their shells and, if they're large, chop the meat.

Melt the butter in your stew pan and sauté the onion and garlic for 3 to 4 minutes. Add the potato, clam broth, half-and-half, and seasonings. Cover and simmer for 5 minutes. Add the clams and brandy, taste for seasoning, and barely simmer for 5 to 10 minutes, or until the clams and potatoes are tender.

◆ Serve with a cucumber and radish salad.

◆ Make a clam pie. Prepare the clams and sauté the onion and garlic as above. Cook the remaining ingredients as above, omitting the half-and-half. Add 3 or 4 chopped hard-cooked eggs. Turn into an 8- or 9-inch pie plate. Make an instant pie crust of 1 cup flour, ¼ teaspoon salt, ¼ cup vegetable oil, and 2 tablespoons milk. Use a fork to stir the ingredients together; then roll out the pastry between sheets of plastic wrap. Place the pie crust over the filling in the pie plate, seal the edges, and make a few small slits in the top for steam to escape. Bake at 425°F. for 12 to 15 minutes.

◆ White Rhône–Hermitage, Crozes-Hermitage, Châteauneuf-du-Pape—makes perfect company for the heartiness of clam stews and chowders. For something a bit lighter, Premier Cru Chablis, Rully, or California Sauvignon Blanc are all possibilities.

Steamed Clams with Vegetables

1 dozen hard-shell clams (littleneck, cherrystone, or Manila)
1 small turnip
1 small onion
1 large carrot
1 clove garlic
¼ cup fresh parsley
¼ cup fresh cilantro
4 tablespoons butter
Black pepper
⅓ cup white wine

Scrub clams thoroughly and rinse under cold running water.

Dice turnip, onion, and carrot. Mince garlic, parsley, and cilantro.

Melt butter in a wide-bottomed pan with a close-fitting lid. Sauté vegetables and herbs over low heat for about 5 minutes, until slightly softened. Season with pepper, add wine and clams, and cover pan tightly. Steam until clams open, about 7 to 10 minutes.

Remove clams and vegetables with a slotted spoon to soup bowls. Ladle on the broth and garnish with additional fresh cilantro if desired.

◆ Serve with Pesto Spaghetti Squash and finish with a good ripe cheese.

◆ Mussels are delicious prepared in the same way and, for a variant in seasoning, add a few strands of saffron to the vegetables when sautéing them.

◆ Crisp, fruity young Loire white wines, like Muscadet, Sancerre, and Pouilly Fumé, are ideal for steamed clams.

Clam and Sausage Chowder

1 dozen hard-shelled clams (littleneck, cherrystone, or Manila)
1 cup dry white wine
¼ pound hot Italian sausage
1 potato, cubed
½ head fennel, sliced crosswise
1 green or red bell pepper, sliced crosswise
1 small onion, sliced in rings
2 cloves garlic, minced
2 large tomatoes, seeded and chopped
2 sprigs fresh oregano, or ½ teaspoon dried oregano
Black and cayenne peppers
⅓ cup chopped fresh Italian parsley

Scrub clams thoroughly and rinse under cold running water. Put with wine in a large saucepan with a tight lid. Steam over medium heat for about 7 to 10 minutes, or until barely open. Remove from heat and set aside.

Slice sausage in chunks and sauté in a large skillet until some fat is released. Add potato and brown with sausage. Add fennel, bell pepper, onion, and garlic, and brown lightly. Add tomatoes, oregano, and peppers.

Strain clam liquid through doubled cheesecloth or a kitchen towel and add the liquid to the vegetables. Cover skillet and simmer gently for 10 minutes, or until potatoes are fork-tender. Add clams in their shells for the last 3 minutes to warm them. Sprinkle with parsley and serve from skillet.

◆ Serve with crusty bread and Sweet Lemon Noodles for dessert.

◆ Clams are also wonderful with cubed pork, as the Portuguese know. Substitute ½ pound boneless pork, cubed, for the sausage and proceed as above.

◆ Try a full-bodied rosé from Tavel, or a light red wine from Provence.

Scallops with Hazelnuts

½ cup hazelnuts, skins on
4 tablespoons butter
1 pound sea scallops
¼ teaspoon ground cumin
⅛ teaspoon ground nutmeg
Salt and black pepper
Fresh lime juice to taste

Chop nuts to medium-fine in a food processor. Heat butter in a large skillet until it begins to brown. Toast nuts in the butter for 1 to 2 minutes.

If scallops are large, slice them in half to make 2 thin rounds. Add scallops, cumin, nutmeg, and seasonings to skillet. Sauté scallops gently for about 2 minutes, or just until they turn opaque (do not overcook). Squeeze a little lime juice over the scallops and serve.

◆ Good with a crisp salad like the Brie-Arugula Salad with Balsamic Cream Dressing or, for color contrast, Hot Beet Salad.

◆ If you like to use scallop shells, mix scallops with a light cream sauce thickened with onion instead of flour. Sauté a small chopped onion in 2 tablespoons butter, add ⅔ cup heavy cream with seasonings, and purée in a blender. Add the scallops to the sauce, place them in a single layer in 4 shells arranged on a cookie sheet or baking pan. Cover with ¼ cup chopped nuts mixed with the same amount of fresh bread crumbs, browned in 3 or 4 tablespoons butter. Bake at 375°F. for 10 to 12 minutes (depending on size), or until the scallops are opaque. Squeeze lime over the tops before serving.

◆ Scallops' sweetness pairs beautifully with white wines that have a trace of sweetness themselves. Look for Vouvray Sec or Dry California Chenin Blanc.

Wok-Smoked Scallops with Green Sauce

1 pound sea scallops
¼ cup black tea leaves
¼ cup brown rice
¼ cup brown sugar

SAUCE:
¼ cup fresh parsley
¼ cup fresh cilantro
2 cloves garlic, mashed
1 tablespoon white wine vinegar
1 tablespoon sour cream
2 tablespoons fresh lime juice
1 teaspoon salt
¼ teaspoon ground cumin
Pinch of cayenne pepper

Cut large scallops in half to make 2 thin rounds. Line a wok with aluminum foil and put the smoking mixture—tea leaves, rice, and sugar—in middle of the foil. Cover tightly with a foil-lined lid and place wok over high heat for 5 minutes. Place scallops in a single layer on a mesh rack or on a rack covered with foil (slit foil in several places so the smoke will come through). Place rack in wok, cover with lid, and smoke over high heat for 5 minutes. Remove from heat and let sit, covered, for 10 minutes.

Prepare sauce by puréeing the ingredients in a blender. Pour sauce on a platter and heap scallops on top of the sauce.

◆ Serve with Apricot Sweet Potatoes or with Wok-Grilled Fennel, cooked in the wok before you cook the scallops.

◆ Almost any kind of shellfish or fish does well with this sort of smoking and this kind of sauce. For an herb flavor without the bother of smoking, sauté the scallops in a little butter and oil and serve with the same sauce.

◆ Smoky Kabinett Rieslings, especially from Rheingau, are great for pan-smoked shellfish.

Scallops in Orange Butter

3 green onions with tops
1 inch-long piece gingerroot, peeled
1 orange
6 tablespoons butter
2 tablespoons dry vermouth
1 pound bay scallops (or sea scallops cut into quarters)
Salt and black and cayenne peppers
Fresh mint for garnish

Cut the onions into 2-inch lengths and shred them. Shred the gingerroot. Grate the orange rind and set aside. Cut the orange in half and scrape out the pulp.

Melt 2 tablespoons of the butter in a small skillet and add the orange pulp, onions, ginger, and vermouth. Barely simmer for 2 or 3 minutes.

Wash the scallops, drain, and pat dry with paper towels. Season well with salt and peppers. Melt the remaining butter until bubbly in a large skillet. Add the scallops and shake them in the pan over high heat to barely cook them through, about 1 minute. Turn scallops into a serving dish and pour the sauce over them. Sprinkle on the orange rind and a few sprigs of fresh mint.

◆ Serve with Zucchini Gratin and end with fresh peaches in champagne.

◆ For a gratin, put the scallops in a shallow baking dish and cover with a mixture of ½ cup fresh bread crumbs, 2 tablespoons minced parsley (or mint), 1 tablespoon minced garlic, and 2 tablespoons chopped walnuts. Top with ¼ pound butter, cut in slices and strewn over the whole. Bake at 450°F. on the top rack of the oven for 6 to 10 minutes.

◆ White Châteauneuf-du-Pape or Crozes-Hermitage are good with scallops, or for a more delicate alternative, try a dry California Chenin Blanc or a Vouvray Sec.

Oyster Cream Stew

1 pint shucked oysters
1 small onion, minced
¼ teaspoon dried thyme
4 tablespoons butter
1 8-ounce bottle clam juice
1 pint heavy cream
Salt, black pepper, and fresh lemon juice
Pinch of grated nutmeg or mace

Drain the oysters over a bowl and save the liquid. Be sure the oysters are free of shell. Sauté the onion and thyme in the butter until tender and scrape into a blender. Add the clam juice and liquefy. Add the oyster liquid, cream, and seasonings and return to the pan. Bring to a simmer and taste for seasoning. (If the liquid has curdled from too-high heat, return it to the blender and liquefy again.) Add the oysters and heat them gently until the edges just begin to curl. Serve in bowls with a grinding of nutmeg on top.

◆ Serve with Sweet Corn Salad and end with a Walnut-Apricot Tart.

◆ For a thicker sauce, boil ¼ cup rice with half a minced onion in 1 pint of clam juice until the rice is tender. Add the oyster liquid, mixed with 3 egg yolks and 2 tablespoons lemon juice. Keep the liquid below a simmer and add the oysters. Cook until the edges just begin to curl. Serve garnished with thin lemon slices.

◆ Muscadet is a traditional partner for oysters, but a somewhat rounder equivalent would be more suitable to the cream: Italian Chardonnay or a Mâcon-Villages would be fine. For more flavor, try an Oregon Chardonnay.

Coconut Shellfish Curry

1 small onion, chopped
2 cloves garlic, minced
1 jalapeño pepper, minced
2 or 3 slices gingerroot, peeled and minced
1 teaspoon paprika
1 tablespoon Madras curry powder
Salt and black and cayenne peppers
2 tablespoons butter
4 plum tomatoes, peeled, seeded, and cubed
2 cups fish stock or clam juice
¼ cup canned sweetened coconut cream
1 to 2 tablespoons fresh lime juice
6 small clams in the shell, well scrubbed
½ pound shrimp, peeled
6 mussels in the shell, well scrubbed
1 tablespoon chopped fresh cilantro

In a large skillet with a lid, sauté the onion, garlic, jalapeño pepper, gingerroot, spices, and seasonings in the butter. Add the tomatoes and the stock, mixed with the coconut cream and lime juice. Bring to a simmer, add the clams, cover, and simmer for 3 minutes. Add the mussels and shrimp, cover, and steam until all the shells open, 5 to 8 minutes. Serve in soup bowls and sprinkle with cilantro.

◆ Serve with plain rice and finish with Avocado-Pineapple Cream.

◆ Use the same curried sauce for other fish, such as fillets of flounder, tilefish, red snapper, halibut, or monkfish. Use only ½ cup of stock and simmer the fish in the sauce, covered, until the fish is just cooked through but doesn't fall apart.

◆ The combination of sweet and sour suggests a wine with an equally ambivalent personality: Alsatian Gewürztraminer or a Riesling from the Rhine or California.

Mussels in Hot Potato Salad

1 quart mussels
½ cup dry white wine
1 clove garlic, minced
¼ cup minced fresh parsley
1 leek
4 new potatoes, with skins
⅓ cup olive oil
2 tablespoons balsamic vinegar
Salt and black pepper
Chives for garnish

Scrub mussels thoroughly, rinse under cold running water, and pull off beards. Put in a large tight-lidded pan with wine, garlic, and parsley. Steam over medium heat for 5 to 8 minutes, or until shells open. Remove pan from heat and set aside.

Cut leek in half just down to the root end, rinse thoroughly to remove sand from inner layers. Cut off and discard root end and most of green top. Slice crosswise.

Pour mussel liquid into a medium saucepan, bring it to a boil. Add leek and new potatoes and boil, covered, about 10 minutes, or until tender. Remove and cool enough to slice potatoes. Place them with the drained leek on a platter.

Remove mussels from their shells, add to leek and sliced potatoes, and dress with a vinaigrette made of the oil, vinegar, and seasonings. Sprinkle with chopped chives.

◆ Serve with Red Pepper-Garlic Soup and follow with Banana Zabaglione.

◆ Turn this into a kind of Salade Niçoise by adding parboiled green beans, black and green olives, hard-cooked eggs, and chunks of grilled tuna.

◆ Crisp, light white wines such as Verdicchio and Village Chablis are fine accompaniments to steamed mussels.

Lobster Tarragon

2 lobsters, 1½ pounds each
1 cup heavy cream
¼ cup Pernod
3 tablespoons chopped fresh tarragon, or 1 teaspoon dried tarragon
Black and cayenne peppers
Fresh lemon juice to taste

Bring several quarts of water to boil in a deep pot and add 1 table-spoon of salt for each quart of water. Plunge the lobsters head down into the pot and cover. Boil for 12 to 15 minutes; then remove the lobsters and run them under cold water until they are cool enough to handle.

Put the lobsters on a cutting board with a well to collect the juices. Cut each lobster in half lengthwise using a sharp knife or kitchen scissors. Cut down the center of the back; then turn the lobster over and repeat on the underside, cutting all the way through the tail meat. Remove the long intestine from the tail, but leave the meat in the shell. Clean the body cavity, discarding the stomach sac, gills, and small legs. Crack claws and remove meat.

Put the green tomalley (liver), the white fat, and any orange coral (roe) into a blender. Pour all of the accumulated juices into the blender and add the cream, Pernod, half of the tarragon, and all of the seasonings. Blend until smooth. Pour into a medium saucepan and bring to a boil. Reduce the sauce until slightly thickened. Pile the claw meat into the cleaned body cavity. Pour the sauce over the tail and claw meat and garnish with the remaining tarragon.

◆ Serve with Yogurt Rice and Cassis sorbet.

◆ For a lobster salad remove all lobster meat from the cooked lobster, cut the tail and claw meat into chunks, and mix with cubes of foie gras pâté and diced raw tomatoes. Put on a bed of arugula or shredded romaine and dress with fresh mayonnaise and lots of tarragon.

◆ Lobster is traditionally considered the best partner for the great full-bodied Chardonnays of California or Burgundy, but the Pernod in this version suggests a lighter alternative: Saint-Véran, Pinot Grigio, or an Alsatian Pinot Gris.

Lobster with Avocado and Tequila

1 large lobster (2 to 3 pounds)
4 tablespoons butter
Salt and black pepper
3 green onions with tops, chopped
¼ cup fish stock or white wine
¼ cup tequila
½ ripe avocado
Rind and juice of 1 lime

Hold live lobster firmly on a cutting board and dispatch it (quickly and humanely) by inserting a strong knife in the slot between the tail and the body and pushing the blade down until it touches the board. Cut up lobster over a wide bowl in order to save all juices. Slit open the underside of the tail with a pair of kitchen scissors and extract the meat. Cut through the underside of the body with scissors and extract any green tomalley (liver) or red coral (roe). Crack claws and legs and extract meat. Cut tail meat in chunks about the size of the claw meat.

Melt butter in medium sauté pan. Season lobster pieces with salt and pepper and sauté with the green onions for 2 minutes. Add lobster juices, fish stock, and tequila, and simmer for 3 or 4 minutes, or until lobster just turns opaque. Remove lobster and pour its liquid and onions into a blender. Add avocado in chunks, plus the lime juice, and purée. Thin sauce if necessary with more tequila. Pour sauce onto a platter, put the lobster on top, and sprinkle it with grated lime rind.

◆ Serve this rich dish with a light salad such as Thai Papaya and end with Jalapeño-Lime Ice.

◆ Lobster and cubes of avocado make a good salad, just as crab and avocado do. Steam the lobster ahead, cut up the meat, combine it with avocado, and minced red onion, and dress it with a lime vinaigrette flavored with fresh cilantro.

◆ Light- to medium-bodied Sauvignon Blancs and Chardonnays from California—provided they aren't too alcoholic—are fine partners for this Southwestern plate.

Soft-Shell Crabs in Black Butter

4 soft-shell crabs
Salt and black and cayenne peppers
¼ cup milk
½ cup flour
2 tablespoons olive oil
4 tablespoons butter
Juice of ½ lemon
3 tablespoons chopped parsley
1 tablespoon drained large capers

Cook the crabs as soon as possible after they've been cleaned. Season them well on both sides and pour the milk over them in a dish. Remove the crabs from the milk and dust them with flour.

Heat the oil and half the butter until bubbly in a large skillet. Cook the crabs over medium heat for 3 to 5 minutes a side, or until crisp and golden. Remove to a warm platter. Add the remaining butter and heat until it just begins to brown. Remove the skillet from the heat, add the remaining ingredients, and pour the sauce over the crabs.

◆ Rice is good to soak up the sauce, but so is toast. A radicchio or endive salad makes a nice contrast.

◆ For a Chinese flavor, sauté the crabs in peanut oil instead of olive oil; then season the sauce with a teaspoon *each* of fermented black beans (available in Asian stores) and gingerroot, a little minced garlic, a chopped green onion (scallion), dry sherry, and soy sauce or clam juice.

◆ This is an excellent opportunity to go for the best dry white you can afford: Puligny-Montrachet, Meursault, or a full-bodied Chardonnay from one of the top wineries of California or Australia.

Salsa Squid

1 pound squid, cleaned
4 tablespoons olive oil
2 tablespoons fresh lime juice
2 teaspoons red or white wine vinegar
1 small red onion, chopped
1 sweet red pepper, chopped
1 tomato, seeded and chopped
1 jalapeño pepper, seeded and minced
¼ cup chopped fresh cilantro
Salt and black pepper

Cut the body of the squid crosswise into rings, leaving the tentacles whole. Heat oil in a large skillet over moderate heat and sauté squid gently for 1 or 2 minutes, just long enough to turn flesh opaque (be careful not to overcook). Add remaining ingredients to squid, adding salt and pepper to taste, and serve at room temperature.

◆ Half the quantity makes a good starter and, like a seviche, tastes great with margaritas. If you serve it as an entrée, accompany it with a soothing carbohydrate, such as Green Rice or Red Lentils.

◆ The same salsa will accommodate a wide variety of additions, such as shrimp and scallops, cubes of grilled tuna, cubes of avocado, quartered hard-cooked eggs, and fresh corn kernels.

◆ Inexpensive sparkling wines from Spain, Australia, and California are every bit as good as beer at extinguishing jalapeño-induced bonfires.

Fish

Red Pepper Salmon
Wood-Smoked Salmon in Orange Butter
Black Pepper Salmon Steaks
Sicilian Swordfish
Asparagus Bass
Smoked Shad and Fiddlehead Ferns
Skillet-Smoked Tuna
Tuna with Tapenade
Roasted Garlic Cod
Carmelized Onion Cod
Walnut-Crusted Flounder
Mako Shark Provençal
Balsamic Bluefish
Fish Chowder with Chickpeas
Coconut Snapper
White Fish with Summer Green Sauce

Red Pepper Salmon

2 sweet red peppers
¼ cup olive oil
½ small red onion, chopped
1 clove garlic, minced
2 anchovy fillets
Black and cayenne peppers
1 pound salmon steaks or fillets

Roast the peppers under a broiler or directly over a gas flame, turning until the skin is charred on all sides. Peel, seed, and chop the flesh coarsely.

In half the oil, sauté the onion and garlic for 2 or 3 minutes in a medium skillet. Put the peppers, onion, garlic, anchovies, and seasonings in a processor or blender and purée. Return to the skillet and keep it warm.

Heat the remaining oil in a large skillet over high heat and brown the salmon on both sides while keeping the inside pink. Add the pan juices to the sauce, pour the sauce onto a platter, and top with the salmon.

◆ Serve with Sesame Eggplant or a red-leaf lettuce salad. End with fresh pears in a chocolate sauce.

◆ Instead of a red sauce, make a classic green sauce of sorrel (or arugula or watercress). Sauté 1 cup of packed green leaves (stems removed) in 4 tablespoons butter until wilted. Purée in a blender and add ½ cup of crème fraîche or heavy cream. Season with pepper and balsamic vinegar or lemon juice.

◆ A full-bodied Côtes du Rhône or Gigondas would be substantial enough to negotiate all the flavors here. If you would rather drink a white, try something from the same region, such as Château-neuf-du-Pape or Crozes-Hermitage. Sauvignon Blanc would be the best choice from California.

Wood-Smoked Salmon in Orange Butter

1 pound salmon fillet, 1½ inches thick
1½ tablespoons olive oil
½ teaspoon chipotle chili, ground
Salt and black pepper

SAUCE:
4 tablespoons butter
Zest and juice of 1 blood orange
¼ to 1 teaspoon sherry or balsamic vinegar

Put a large handful of hardwood chips in a container of cold water and let soak about 30 minutes.

Meanwhile, cut the salmon fillet in half crosswise and marinate in the oil, chili, and seasonings for 30 minutes.

Line a wok or heavy skillet with aluminum foil, heap the chips on the foil, cover tightly with a foil-lined lid and heat over a high flame for 10 minutes. When the chips are smoking, remove the lid, place the salmon on a rack and put the rack over the chips. Cover and smoke over medium heat for 10 minutes (do not remove the lid). Take the pan off the heat and let it sit, covered, for another 15 minutes.

Just before serving, heat the butter until bubbly in a small saucepan and whisk in the orange juice and zest, beating vigorously. Add a few drops of sherry or vinegar to taste.

◆ Look for a wine that will stand up to the smokiness of the cooking method and the fruitiness of the orange—a Dolcetto from Italy, slightly chilled, will a marriage make.

Black Pepper Salmon Steaks

2 tablespoons black peppercorns
1 teaspoon Szechuan peppercorns
1 pound salmon steaks or fillets
Salt to taste
1 tablespoon sesame oil
¼ cup dry sherry

Crush or grind both kinds of peppercorns coarsely and press into salmon on both sides. Salt lightly. Heat a wok or heavy cast-iron skillet over high heat until smoking. Add oil and then salmon. Sear salmon on both sides, lower heat, then add sherry carefully because it will flame. Cooking time depends on thickness of steak or fillet. If salmon is less than an inch thick, cook it less than 2 to 3 minutes a side.

◆ Serve with Appled Eggplant, Turnip-Pear Purée, or Tahini Broccoli.

◆ Different spices, used the same way, will produce different but also delicious effects. Coarsely grind a mixture of cumin and coriander, or fennel seeds. Or, try a dusting of allspice or Chinese 5-spice powder.

◆ Spicy salmon loves a refreshing, young rosé, like a Rosé d'Anjou or Vin Gris de Pinot Noir, to cool its flames.

Sicilian Swordfish

1 pound swordfish (2 1-inch-thick steaks)
¼ cup olive oil
2 cloves garlic, minced
Fresh thyme, sage, and parsley, chopped
Salt and black and cayenne peppers
3 anchovy fillets, mashed
½ lemon
1 tablespoon drained capers

Marinate the steaks, chilled, in a plastic bag in the oil, garlic, half the fresh herbs, and salt and peppers, for as long as you can (30 minutes to 6 hours).

Brown the fish on both sides in a large hot skillet (add more oil if needed), lower the heat slightly, and cook until the flesh inside turns from translucent to opaque, 5 to 8 minutes. *Don't* overcook or the fish will be tough and dry. Put the steaks on a warm plate.

Stir the mashed anchovies into the pan juices and squeeze in the lemon juice. Add the capers and the remaining fresh herbs. Swirl and pour the sauce over the fish.

◆ Good with a Roasted Pepper Salad and a plain shell pasta.

◆ Broil or bake a swordfish steak by coating it in oil and then a mixture of garlic and fresh or dried herbs, such as rosemary and thyme. Broil close to the heat source for 3 to 5 minutes on each side or in a 450°F. oven for 10 minutes. Serve with a garnish of Mediterranean black olives chopped together with garlic and lemon rind.

◆ A good California Chardonnay will match the richness of the dish. For an interesting alternative, try a Chardonnay or Sauvignon Blanc from Australia.

Asparagus Bass

1 pound striped bass, or tilefish, whitefish, etc., fillets
Salt and black and cayenne peppers
2 tablespoons fresh lemon juice
4 tablespoons butter
1 pound asparagus
2 tablespoons sour cream

Season the fish and sprinkle it with lemon juice; then dot with 2 tablespoons of the butter and bake in a buttered pan at 350°F. for 5 to 10 minutes.

Meanwhile, wash the asparagus and break off the tough ends. Peel the stems and then chop them to an inch below the tips. Reserve the tips and put the stems in a small saucepan and add salted water to cover. Boil until the stems are very tender. Remove with a slotted spoon to a blender. Put the asparagus tips in the same water and simmer until just tender, 3 to 4 minutes. Remove to a warm dish.

Pour off all but 1 cup of the asparagus water and boil down to 2 tablespoons. Add to the blender. Add the pan juices of the baked fish along with the sour cream to the blender and purée until smooth. Arrange the fish on a warm platter, pour on the sauce, and arrange the asparagus tips on top.

◆ Serve with boiled new potatoes or Garlic Roast Potatoes. End with bananas sautéed in butter, molasses, and rum.

◆ Make a different kind of green sauce with spinach and watercress or arugula. Wilt 2 cups of packed leaves in 2 tablespoons of butter. Purée in a blender with 1 cup of yogurt. Add lemon juice to taste.

◆ The special taste of asparagus is best complemented by Sauvignon Blanc from California or Italy, or its equivalent in a white Graves, Sancerre, or Pouilly Fumé.

Smoked Shad and Fiddlehead Ferns

1 pound shad fillets
Salt and black pepper
2 chipotle chilies
¼ pound fresh fiddlehead ferns
2 tablespoons olive oil
Squeeze of fresh lemon

Season the shad with salt and pepper on both sides and refrigerate until ready to cook.

Put a large handful of hardwood chips with the two chipotle chilies in a container of cold water and let soak 30 minutes. Line a wok or heavy skillet with aluminum foil and heap the chips and the chilies on top of the foil. Cover tightly with a foil-lined lid and heat over a high flame for 10 minutes. Remove the lid, place the fish on a rack, and place the rack over the chips. Cover again tightly and smoke the fish over medium heat for 5 minutes (do not remove the lid). Remove the pan from the heat and let it sit, covered, for another 5 minutes.

Meanwhile, steam the ferns in a bamboo steamer or in a rack over boiling water for 10 to 15 minutes (large ones for 20). Put the ferns in a colander and run cold water over them to retain their color and crispness. Mix with the olive oil and lemon, and arrange the ferns around the shad.

◆ Try pairing this smoked shad with a good Alsatian Pinot Gris. The fruit and roundness of this wine should bring out the better qualities of shad. Another good choice would be one of the terrific California Viogniers.

Skillet–Smoked Tuna

1 tablespoon peanut oil
1 pound tuna, 1½-inches thick
3 tablespoons crushed coriander seeds
1 teaspoon cumin seeds
¼ cup black tea leaves
¼ cup brown rice
¼ cup brown sugar
¼ cup fresh cilantro, chopped
3 or 4 slices gingerroot, peeled and minced
2 tablespoons butter, softened
Fresh lemon juice to taste

In a very hot wok or heavy skillet, heat the peanut oil, sear the tuna quickly on both sides, and remove. Wipe out the pan and line it with aluminum foil. Spread it with a mixture of the seeds, tea, rice, and sugar. Line a wok cover or skillet lid with foil. Place a rack, large enough to hold the fish, inside the wok or skillet on top of the mixture. Cover and heat over high heat for 5 minutes. Place the tuna on the rack and cover again. Turn the heat to low and smoke the fish for 10 minutes. Remove from the heat and let sit for 10 minutes with the lid on.

Mix the cilantro and ginger with the butter and lemon juice. Garnish the smoked fish with the butter.

◆ Serve with Hot Pear Salad in Chinese Hot Sauce.

◆ Marinate tuna or other fish fillets (mackerel, shad, eel, or small whole fish, such as snapper or trout), in a fresh cilantro sauce of ¼ cup cilantro, 1 clove garlic, 2 slices gingerroot, a pinch of cumin seeds and cayenne pepper, a dash of fresh lemon juice, and ¼ cup oil for 40 minutes. Smoke as above without browning the fish first, or broil the fish without smoking.

◆ Try a white Graves or a full-bodied California Sauvignon Blanc to complement the smoked flavor, or else a fairly dry Riesling from California or the Rhine for an interesting alternative.

Tuna with Tapenade

1 pound tuna (2 1-inch-thick steaks)

TAPENADE:
¼ cup olive oil
½ cup green olives, Mediterranean style
1 clove garlic, mashed
2 teaspoons mashed anchovies, or anchovy paste
1 teaspoon Dijon mustard
1 tablespoon fresh lemon juice
1 tablespoon chopped fresh Italian parsley

Brush tuna on both sides with a little of the oil. Heat a wok or heavy skillet over high heat until smoking. Sear tuna on both sides, about 3 minutes per side to keep it rare. Remove fish and cut it into thin slices.

Make tapenade by puréeing the remaining oil and all the tapenade ingredients in a blender. If mixture is too thick, add more oil (or a little white wine) to thin it.

Mound the tapenade in the middle of a platter and surround it with slices of tuna.

◆ Serve with Kale and Red Pepper Sauté or Red Lentils.

◆ For an unusual flavor, use a miso paste with toasted Nori seaweed (available in health food stores). In a blender, purée 2 tablespoons miso and 1 toasted Nori sheet with 2 tablespoons oil, 1 tablespoon vinegar, 1 teaspoon soy sauce, 1 teaspoon chopped ginger, and ¼ teaspoon toasted and ground Szechuan peppercorns.

◆ Sharp, fruity red wines, such as Chinon and Bourgueil, go beautifully with rare tuna.

Roasted Garlic Cod

15 cloves garlic, unpeeled
½ cup olive oil
½ teaspoon Dijon mustard
2 teaspoons fresh lemon juice or white wine vinegar
Salt and black pepper
1 pound cod steaks or fillets (about 1-inch thick)
½ cup white wine
Fresh parsley sprigs for garnish

Brush garlic with a little of the oil and roast it in aluminum foil at 375°F. for 20 minutes. Squeeze garlic flesh from skins and blend with oil, mustard, lemon juice, and seasonings until smooth, making a thick mayonnaise.

Poach cod in the wine in a large covered skillet over moderate heat for 6 to 10 minutes, or until cod is just fork-tender. Remove cod to a serving platter. Thin garlic sauce in blender by adding ¼ cup of poaching liquid. Pour sauce over the cod. Garnish with fresh parsley.

◆ Serve with boiled new potatoes and a light salad, followed by good cheese and fruit.

◆ Another complement to cod is leeks. Clean 4 leeks well, cut in half crosswise, then lengthwise, and slice into thin strips (julienne). Stew in a skillet in 6 tablespoons butter for 6 to 8 minutes to soften. Remove half the leeks, add cod, cover with remaining leeks, season, cover skillet with a lid, and steam cod for 6 to 10 minutes.

◆ Serve with a crisp, light white wine such as a Trebbiano or Alsatian Sylvaner.

Caramelized Onion Cod

3 large onions
¼ teaspoon ground turmeric
1¼ teaspoon ground ginger
2 tablespoons olive oil
2 tablespoons butter
1 pound cod (2 1½-inch-thick steaks)
Salt and black pepper

In a medium heavy skillet, sauté the onions, turmeric, and ginger over low heat in the oil and butter until caramel colored, about 30 to 40 minutes. Season the cod with the salt and pepper and let sit while the onions are cooking.

Arrange a layer of the onions in a baking dish, put the cod on top, and cover with another layer of onions. Cover the dish with a tight lid or aluminum foil, sealing the edges. Bake at 400°F. for 8 to 12 minutes.

◆ Serve with Yogurt Rice and steamed baby carrots.

◆ Bake cod or other white fish (halibut, haddock, or tilefish) in a cup of heavy cream with a cup of minced onions, some minced garlic, and fresh basil or mint. To thicken the sauce, purée the cream, onion, garlic, and pan juices in a blender. Add a smoked mussel to the blender for a darker flavor.

◆ A moderately priced Chardonnay from California or Italy would be most suitable, or else a white Rully or Mâcon-Villages.

Walnut-Crusted Flounder

1 pound flounder fillets
Salt and black and cayenne peppers
½ cup walnuts, ground
1 tablespoon each of butter and olive oil

Season fillets on both sides with salt and peppers. Press walnuts into fillets on both sides, as if breading them. Heat butter and oil in a large skillet over moderate heat, add fillets, and brown for 3 to 4 minutes on one side. Turn and brown the other side 1 or 2 minutes only, or until fish has just turned opaque.

◆ Because there is no sauce, you might serve this with a pasta such as Pasta with Artichokes and Olives or Penne with Charred Vegetables.

◆ Almonds or pecans can also be used as a coating for the fish. For an unusual variant, try ground sunflower or pumpkin seeds. Be careful to keep the heat low enough so as not to burn nuts or seeds.

◆ Barrel-fermented Chardonnays from California and Australia, with their pronounced toastiness, complement the nutty flavors in this simple but tasty fish dish.

Mako Shark Provençal

6 cloves garlic
1 sweet red pepper
2 shallots
2 tablespoons olive oil
2 sprigs fresh rosemary, or ½ teaspoon dried rosemary
1 pound mako shark steaks
Salt and black pepper
1 tomato, seeded and chopped
½ cup fish stock
1 cup dry red wine
Fresh rosemary sprigs for garnish

Peel garlic, halve and seed red pepper, and peel shallots. Put olive oil in a baking pan large enough to hold the fish, add vegetables and roll them in the oil, sprinkle with rosemary, and roast at 400°F. for 15 to 20 minutes. Remove pan and lower heat to 350°F.

Brush fish with the olive oil in the pan. Heat a wok or cast-iron skillet until smoking and sear the fish quickly on both sides. Season with salt and pepper and put in baking pan with roasted vegetables. Add tomato, stock, and wine, and bake at 350°F. for 8 to 10 minutes, or until fish is fork-tender.

Remove steaks to a serving dish until they are cool enough to trim out the bone and remove skin. Slice crosswise and surround with roasted vegetables. Garnish with sprigs of rosemary and serve in soup bowls.

◆ Finish the meal with Jalapeño-Lime Ice or a bowl of fresh fruit.

◆ Since shark is a fish that can take strong flavors, try braising it with lemons and onions. Sear it first or not, as you choose, then add it to a baking pan in which a thinly sliced lemon and red onion have cooked in the red wine.

◆ Look for light, fruity red wines from Provence and Northern Italy, such as Bandol and Dolcetta d'Alba.

Balsamic Bluefish

1 pound bluefish fillets
1 tablespoon olive oil
Salt and black pepper
2 green onions with tops, chopped
¼ cup red or white wine
1 tablespoon balsamic vinegar
6 or 7 fresh basil leaves

Roll fillets in the oil in a nonmetal baking dish and season with salt and pepper on both sides. Sprinkle with the onions, add wine, vinegar, and half the basil. Cover dish tightly with aluminum foil and bake at 350°F. for 8 to 10 minutes, depending on thickness of the fillets. Garnish with remaining basil.

◆ Serve with Thai Papaya Salad or Red Lentils.

◆ Because of its oil, bluefish does well grilled or broiled. If you have time and like Chinese flavors, before grilling, marinate fish for half an hour in ¼ cup soy sauce, 1 tablespoon sesame oil, 1 or 2 slices fresh gingerroot (chopped), and ½ teaspoon Japanese wasabi mustard.

◆ Try light, acidic white wines with little or no trace of wood, such as New York Chardonnay and Alto Pinot Grigio.

Fish Chowder with Chickpeas

½ head fennel, sliced, with green tops
1 sweet red pepper, seeded and chopped
1 small red chili pepper, seeded and diced
1 small onion, chopped
1 clove garlic, minced
Pinch of saffron
2 to 3 slices gingerroot, minced
2 tablespoons olive oil
1 pound monkfish, or similar sturdy fish
Salt and black pepper
1½ cups cooked chickpeas
2 cups fish stock or clam juice
1 cup plain yogurt

Put fennel, sweet and red chili peppers, onion, garlic, saffron, and ginger in a large saucepan with the olive oil. Sauté the vegetables gently for 2 to 3 minutes, to slightly soften.

Cut monkfish into 2-inch cubes and add to saucepan. Season lightly.

Put half the chickpeas in a blender with half the stock and purée until smooth. Add the purée with remaining stock, chickpeas, and yogurt to saucepan. Bring liquid to the simmer and cook fish 3 or 4 minutes over low heat, or until just fork-tender.

◆ Serve with an Indian bread such as nan or chapati and end the meal with Grape Freezies or Gingered Figs.

◆ Monkfish is also good with lentils. Substitute 1½ cups cooked yellow lentils for the chickpeas and proceed as above.

◆ Try this Indian-inspired seafood soup with a medium-bodied German Riesling, such as a Spätlese Halbtrocken or Trocken from the Rheinhessen.

Coconut Snapper

2 tablespoons olive oil
1 small onion, chopped
1 clove garlic, minced
1 jalapeño pepper, seeded and minced
2 or 3 slices gingerroot, minced
¼ cup canned sweetened coconut cream
½ cup fish stock or clam juice
Salt and pepper
1 pound red snapper fillets
2 tablespoons fresh lime juice

In a large skillet, heat oil and sauté onion, garlic, jalapeño, and ginger gently until softened. Stir in coconut cream and fish stock. Season snapper fillets and add to the mixture in the skillet. Spoon some of the sauce over the fish. Cover pan and poach fish gently over low heat 4 to 7 minutes, or until just fork-tender. Squeeze lime over the fish and remove fish to a serving platter. Pour sauce over the fish.

◆ Serve with Tropical Fruit Salad and lemon squares for dessert.

◆ Since snapper is a beautiful fish to serve whole, try steaming it, Asian style, in a wok with ½ cup water in the bottom. Make 3 deep parallel cuts on each side of the fish. Place the fish on a dish that will fit into the wok, with flavorings on top, and cover tightly. Use the same flavorings as above, substituting green onions for onion and diluting the coconut cream with lime juice, omitting the stock. Cover with a tight lid and steam 15 to 20 minutes for a 1½- to 2-pound fish, 20 to 25 for a 3-pounder.

◆ Gewürztraminers, which often suggest coconut and other tropical fruits, pair well with exotic, slightly sweet preparations. Look for examples from Northern Italy and the cooler parts of California.

White Fish with Summer Green Sauce

1 pound white fish fillets, such as cod, flounder, haddock, halibut
2 tablespoons olive oil
2 green onions with tops, chopped
4 cloves garlic, roasted in their skins
¼ cup basil leaves
4 sprigs parsley
1 cup fish stock
¼ cup plain yogurt
Salt and black pepper

Sauté, grill, bake, or steam the fish fillets.

Meanwhile, make the sauce. In a small skillet, sauté the onions in the oil for 2 to 3 minutes, then put the mixture into a blender with the roasted garlic cloves (skins removed) and the remaining ingredients. Blend until smooth, then return the purée to the skillet and heat until it has thickened slightly.

◆ Something white and fresh—a grassy wine with a hint of the earth—is called for here to accompany the summer greens. Ferrari-Carano makes a wonderful fumé blanc that's not difficult to obtain.

Birds

Avocado-Lime Chicken
Turkish Walnut Chicken
Peanut Chicken Legs
Coconut Chicken with Lemongrass
Barbados Chicken
Chicken Guacamole Tortillas
Turkey Scallopine
Turkey Tonnato
Roasted Turkey Thigh
Marmalade Duck
Duck Breasts with Black Bean Sauce
Gin Quail
Pumpkin-Seed Quail
Squab and Rabe

Avocado-Lime Chicken

2 boned chicken breasts
Salt and black and cayenne peppers
¾ cup heavy cream
¼ teaspoon ground cumin
½ teaspoon ground coriander
½ ripe avocado, peeled and cubed
Rind and juice of 2 limes

Skin the breasts, flatten them slightly (a rolling pin or a heavy jar will do it), and slice them lengthwise into ½-inch-wide strips. Season them well with the salt and peppers. In a large skillet, bring the cream to a boil with the cumin and coriander, add the chicken, and barely simmer 1 to 2 minutes each side. Remove the chicken slices to a warm plate. Boil the cream to thicken it, add the avocado cubes, and lime juice to taste. Pour the sauce over the chicken and sprinkle with the grated rind.

◆ This super-quick dish is good cold or hot. It goes well served over rice and with a tomato vinaigrette salad.

◆ Make chicken slices in a pâte-cream sauce. Purée in a blender ½ cup heavy cream, ¼ cup chicken stock, 2 tablespoons foie gras pâté (or 2 chicken livers cut into pieces and sautéed lightly in butter), ½ teaspoon balsamic vinegar, and lemon juice to taste. Pour the sauce in a skillet and simmer as above. If you like, garnish the slices with cubes of foie gras.

◆ A dry white with good acidity will help to balance the avocado: Sancerre, Pouilly Fumé, white Graves, or Sauvignon Blanc from California. New York Chardonnay is another possibility.

Turkish Walnut Chicken

2 boned chicken breasts
2 tablespoons walnut oil
Black and cayenne peppers
1 small onion, finely chopped
½ cup dry white wine
1 tablespoon fresh lemon juice
1 cup walnuts
Paprika

Coat the chicken breasts with half the walnut oil and season them well on both sides with the peppers. In a large skillet, sauté the onion in the remaining oil until transparent. Add the wine and chicken, cover tightly, and simmer over very low heat for 6 to 10 minutes, turning the chicken once. Cut into the breast at its thickest part to test for doneness. The chicken should just lose its translucence—don't overcook.

Pour the pan juices into a blender, add the lemon juice and walnuts, and purée. Thin if necessary with a little more wine, or with yogurt or cream. Spread the sauce over the breasts and sprinkle with paprika.

◆ Serve with Sesame Eggplant and finish with a fresh fruit salad sprinkled with cumin seeds.

◆ For deep-fried walnut chicken, cut the breasts in chunks and season. Dip them in a batter of 2 egg whites beaten with 1½ tablespoons cornstarch or arrowroot. Roll them in 1 cup ground nuts, pressing the nuts in all around. Refrigerate for 30 minutes. Heat 2 cups of peanut or other vegetable oil in a wok or heavy skillet until hot but not smoking (350°F.) and fry the chicken chunks quickly, two or three at a time. Drain on paper towels.

◆ Two directions are possible here: either Italian, Oregon or New York Chardonnay to go with the lemon and white wine, or a light red Burgundy, such as Mercurey or Côte de Beaune-Villages to bring out the flavor of the walnuts.

Peanut Chicken Legs

2 chicken legs with thighs attached
2 tablespoons peanut oil
1 clove garlic, mashed
1 tablespoon soy sauce
3 or 4 slices gingerroot, peeled and minced
1 tablespoon white wine vinegar
Hot red pepper flakes or cayenne pepper
¼ cup dry sherry, vermouth, or chicken stock
2 tablespoons crunchy peanut butter
1 tablespoon salted peanuts for garnish

In a medium skillet, brown the legs on both sides in the peanut oil over high heat. Add the remaining ingredients, except the peanut butter and peanuts. Cover the skillet, lower the heat, and cook chicken until tender, 25 to 30 minutes. Turn the chicken at least once. Remove the chicken to a warm serving platter.

Stir the peanut butter into the pan juices. Thin with sherry if the sauce is too thick. Pour the sauce over the chicken and sprinkle with peanuts. Serve hot, at room temperature, or cold.

◆ Good with a crisp salad of Jerusalem artichokes or string beans.

◆ Baked parmesan chicken legs. Dip the legs in ¼ cup melted butter seasoned with Worcestershire sauce and Dijon mustard. Roll the legs in 1 cup fresh bread crumbs mixed with ¼ cup *each* of grated Parmesan cheese and minced parsley. Season with salt and pepper and bake at 350°F. for 50 to 60 minutes.

◆ Try a chilled bottle of Beaujolais-Villages (preferably from a top producer like Duboeuf) or, for a white, California Riesling.

Coconut Chicken with Lemongrass

1 tablespoon vegetable oil
Salt and black pepper
1½ pounds chicken thighs and legs
4 green onions with tops, chopped
2 cloves garlic, minced
1 small fresh red or green chili pepper, seeded and minced
1 teaspoon ground coriander
½ teaspoon turmeric
½ teaspoon powdered lemongrass, or 1 fresh blade (see Note)
1 tomato or sweet red pepper, seeded and chopped
¼ cup canned sweetened coconut cream
¾ cup chicken stock
2 tablespoons fresh lime juice, or to taste

Heat oil in a large skillet, season chicken, and brown it on all sides. Add onions, garlic, chili, coriander, and turmeric and sauté for 3 or 4 minutes, until softened.

Add remaining ingredients, except for lime juice, lower heat, and cover pan. Simmer gently for 20 to 25 minutes, or until chicken is fork-tender. Remove from heat, taste sauce, and add lime juice accordingly.

◆ Serve with plain rice or a mix of rice and lentils.

◆ An easy way to cook a whole chicken is to use the same flavorings as above, but instead of sautéing chicken pieces, brown chicken as above, then braise in a covered earthenware pot, such as a Schlemmertopf; or, wrap tightly in banana leaves in aluminum foil.

◆ Try with sparkling Rieslings from Germany (called Sekt) or Alsace (called Crémant d'Alsace).

Note: Dried lemongrass is available at most health food stores in the form of lemongrass tea.

Barbados Chicken

4 chicken pieces, for frying
Salt and black pepper
Flour
2 tablespoons butter
2 oranges
2 teaspoons Dijon mustard
2 or 3 dashes of Tabasco sauce
2 tablespoons orange marmalade
2 tablespoons dark rum

Season chicken well on all sides and roll in the flour. Heat butter in a large skillet and sauté the chicken until evenly browned, about 6 or 10 minutes.

Grate rind of 1 orange and squeeze its juice into a cup. Mix in mustard, Tabasco, marmalade, and rum and adjust this particular mixture of sweet and hot to your taste. (Add lemon if too sweet.) Add sauce to chicken, cover skillet, and simmer 10 to 25 minutes (depending on size), until chicken is tender. Use second orange, peeled and segmented, for garnish.

◆ Serve with Chinese Greens with Pesto or Brie-Arugula Salad with Balsamic Cream Dressing.

◆ Enlarge the Barbados reference by frying the chicken with a peeled and sliced plantain, or with a firm sliced banana, browned in a separate pan and used as garnish.

◆ This sweet, spicy dish calls for a tall, cool bottle of Kabinett Riesling from the Rhein, or a thirst-quenching white Zinfandel.

Chicken Guacamole Tortillas

1 pair chicken breasts (about 1 pound), boned and skinned
Salt and black and cayenne peppers to taste
½ teaspoon ground cumin
1 tablespoon olive oil

GUACAMOLE:
1 ripe avocado
1 jalapeño or serrano pepper, seeded and minced
½ small red onion, chopped
1 clove garlic, minced
1 small tomato, seeded and diced
2 tablespoons chopped fresh cilantro
Salt and black and cayenne peppers
Fresh lime juice to taste
2 large flour tortillas
½ cup sour cream

Season chicken breasts on both sides with salt, peppers, and cumin, and in a large skillet sauté in hot oil 3 to 4 minutes on each side, until golden. Remove and slice thin.

Make guacamole by mashing avocado, adding other ingredients, and seasoning to taste with salt, peppers, and lime juice.

Lay half the chicken slices in one of the tortillas, cover with half the guacamole, and roll up tortilla. Repeat. Serve with sour cream on the side for dipping.

◆ For a big meal, serve with Fresh Corn Tamale Pie and end with Mango-Chili Cream.

◆ For another version, lay chicken slices on flat tortillas, cover with Poblano Sauce (see Charred Shrimp Poblano), topped with grated Monterey Jack cheese, and serve open-faced without rolling the tortillas.

◆ Try California Sauvignon Blancs that have been blended with some Sémillon for added richness.

Turkey Scallopine

1 fresh turkey breast (about ¾ pound)
Salt and black pepper
¼ cup heavy cream
⅓ cup fresh bread crumbs
⅓ cup grated Parmesan cheese
1 tablespoon each of olive oil and butter
¼ cup Madeira, Marsala, Port, or sherry

Slice breast crosswise and pound each slice thin with a mallet or thick plate edge. Season well, dip each slice in cream, bread crumbs, and then cheese to coat both sides.

Heat oil and butter in a large skillet and brown turkey over moderate heat, about 1 minute on each side (for ¼-inch slices), or until just cooked through. Don't overcook. Remove to a platter. Add wine and cook over high heat for 1 minute, stirring in all pan juices. Pour sauce over turkey.

◆ Serve with Turnip-Pear Purée.

◆ Prepackaged turkey breast is undervalued because it is convenient and cheap, but for those very reasons it's good to use in a variety of ways. One way is to braise it whole, in a small covered casserole, with soy, ginger, chili oil, and Chinese vegetables such as straw mushrooms, fresh water chestnuts, and strips of sweet red pepper.

◆ Try a QbA Riesling from the Mosel, or a light Riesling from Washington State.

Turkey Tonnato

1 pound turkey cutlets (¼-inch-thick breast slices)
2 tablespoons olive oil
¼ cup dry white wine
¼ cup canned tuna, drained
2 anchovy fillets
2 tablespoons fresh lemon juice
2 tablespoons mayonnaise
½ cup plain yogurt
Black pepper
2 tablespoons large capers, drained

In a large skillet, sauté the turkey slices quickly on both sides in the olive oil, about 1 to 2 minutes on each side. Put on a serving platter. Pour the pan juices into a blender with all the remaining ingredients, except the capers. Purée to make the tuna-cream sauce (*tonnato*, as the Italians say) and pour the sauce over the slices. Sprinkle with the capers.

◆ Serve with an Italian flat bread like foccacia and a fava bean salad.

◆ The same sauce is traditional with cold veal slices, but if you like the combination of tuna and turkey, a nifty cold dish is made by piling turkey slices (sautéed as above or leftover from a roast or cut from a smoked turkey) with tuna tartare. Buy ¼ pound fresh tuna. Chop it coarsely with a little onion, garlic, anchovy, and parsley. Season it with fresh lemon juice and pepper, brandy if wanted, and sprinkle it with capers.

◆ A Mâcon-Villages would suit well here, or a white Rully for more flavor. Other possibilities include Chardonnays from Italy, Oregon, or New York.

Roasted Turkey Thigh

1 1½-pound turkey thigh, or 2 smaller ones
½ small onion, diced
1 tablespoon olive oil
½ cup spinach leaves, packed
¼ cup raisins
Salt and black and cayenne peppers
¼ cup orange marmalade
1 teaspoon balsamic vinegar

Remove the bone from the thigh so that you can roll the meat in one piece around the stuffing.

Sauté the onion in the oil until softened, then mix in the spinach, raisins, and seasonings.

Season the turkey on both sides, lay in the stuffing where the bone was and roll the meat around it. Place the turkey roll on aluminum foil, seam-side down, and roll the foil around it. Bake at 350°F. for about 45 minutes.

Meanwhile, put the marmalade in a small saucepan with the vinegar and heat it just enough to melt the marmalade. Open up the foil and brush the skin with the glaze. Brown the glazed skin at 400°F. for about 15 minutes. Let rest a few minutes, then cut the thigh in half crosswise or into thick slices.

◆ A traditional pairing won't make any enemies here—for example, an Oregon Chardonnay. Something slightly different but equally suitable would be an Arneis from the Piedmont of Italy.

Marmalade Duck

1 4- to 5-pound fresh duck, cut into pieces
Salt and black and cayenne peppers
½ cup bitter orange marmalade
2 tablespoons fresh lemon juice
1 tablespoon Dijon mustard
1 navel orange, thinly sliced

Remove all the excess fat from the duck that you can. Prick the skin of the breasts and thighs with a fork all over to release the fat when cooking. Season well with the salt and peppers.

Mix the marmalade with the lemon and mustard. Coat the breast and thighs with the marmalade mixture and place on a rack in a roasting pan. Roast at 375°F. for 15 minutes. Remove the breast. Prick the skin of the thighs again and let them continue to roast another 15 to 20 minutes.

Put the breasts and thighs skin-side up on aluminum foil or a broiler pan, heat the broiler and broil the meat for 5 to 10 minutes to crisp the skin and complete the cooking. Put the orange slices over the top.

◆ Serve with Fresh Potato Chips and end with dried figs and walnuts.

◆ Do a duck sauté. Prick the skin thoroughly. Sauté the meat in a hot skillet, skin-side down. Remove the breasts after 5 minutes. Turn the thighs and brown on the other side. Pour off the fat. Add ½ cup good barbecue sauce thinned with white wine and ½ cup Mediterranean green olives. Simmer the thighs until tender, covered. Add the breasts just before serving.

◆ Something on the sweeter side will complement the marmalade, such as California Riesling, Mosel Spätlese, or Gewürztraminer from Alsace. For a suitable red, try a Mercurey, Santenay, or Chassagne-Montrachet from Burgundy.

Duck Breasts with Black Bean Sauce

2 whole duck breasts (4 pieces)
Black pepper
2 tablespoons peanut oil

SAUCE:
1 tablespoon peanut oil
2 cloves garlic, minced
4 to 5 slices gingerroot, minced
2 tablespoons fermented black beans, chopped
⅓ cup dry sherry
1 teaspoon sugar
½ teaspoon soy sauce

Season breasts with pepper and sear in 2 tablespoons oil in a large heavy skillet, browning about 2 minutes on each side to keep them rare within. Remove duck to a platter and cut each breast into thin slices.

Heat 1 tablespoon peanut oil in same skillet; sauté garlic, ginger, and beans 1 to 2 minutes. Add sherry, sugar, and soy sauce, scrape in any pan juices, and pour sauce over the duck.

◆ Good with Chinese Greens with Pesto or Tahini Broccoli.

◆ Duck takes as well to Southwest flavors as to Chinese, so try the same duck method with a Poblano Sauce, using ¼ cup chicken stock as a base (see Charred Shrimp Poblano).

◆ The slight sweetness in this dish makes a fruity red wine such as Beaujolais or California Gamay feel right at home.

Gin Quail

2 fresh quail
Salt and black and cayenne peppers
Flour
2 tablespoons butter
2 tablespoons olive oil
2 or 3 bay leaves, crushed
6 juniper berries, crushed
¼ cup gin
½ cup dry white wine

Split each quail with a knife or poultry shears along the back and flatten it with your hands. Season the birds well and dust with flour. Heat the butter and oil with the bay and juniper. Brown the quail on both sides; then lower the heat and sauté until tender, 3 to 4 minutes. Warm the gin, pour it over the birds and flame them with a match. Remove the birds to a serving platter. Add the wine to the pan juices, reduce rapidly, and pour over the birds.

◆ Serve with toast points or Nutted Wild Rice and young dandelion or other sharp greens.

◆ Roast the quail whole by stuffing each with 2 or 3 oysters, 3 tablespoons butter, and chopped parsley. Season the outside with salt and pepper, wrap each bird in 2 or 3 strips of bacon, and put breast-side up in a roasting pan. Roast at 450°F. for 10 minutes, or until the bacon is crisp. Remove the bacon and brown the birds another 5 minutes. Crumble the bacon over the top for serving.

◆ This calls for a wine with plenty of flavor that isn't too heavy on the palate: Mercurey, Santenay, or a Savigny from Burgundy, Vacqueyras from the Rhône, or a red Rioja from Spain. If you like a more full-bodied red, look for an Oregon Pinot Noir or a young St. Emilion.

Pumpkin-Seed Quail

4 quail
Salt and black pepper
Flour and cornmeal, mixed
2 tablespoons each of olive oil and butter
½ cup pumpkin seeds
2 jalapeño peppers, charred (see Note)
1 clove garlic, minced
¼ onion, chopped
¼ teaspoon ground cumin
1⅓ cups chicken stock
2 sprigs cilantro for garnish

Split each quail along the back, spread it open, and flatten. Clip off the backbone with a pair of kitchen shears. Season birds on both sides with salt and pepper and dust with a mixture of flour and cornmeal.

Heat oil and butter in a large heavy skillet, sear quail on both sides, lower heat and sauté 3 to 4 minutes, until tender. Remove and keep warm.

In same skillet, toast pumpkin seeds 3 or 4 minutes (cover the skillet partially because the seeds will pop up; stir them once or twice to prevent burning). Remove seeds to a blender with the jalapeños. Brown garlic and onion in same pan, add cumin and chicken stock and scrape mixture into blender. Add any juices from reserved quail. Purée and pour sauce onto a platter, lay quail on top, and garnish with cilantro.

◆ Serve with Appled Eggplant and finish with Chocolate-Chili Cream.

◆ Quail take well to wok-smoking (see Wok-Smoked Trout). Season and smoke whole quail for the same time as the trout.

◆ Oregon Pinot Noir or red Burgundy from the Côte de Beaune are great with small birds.

Note: Char peppers by holding them with a pair of tongs over a direct flame until their skins blacken on all sides. Remove stems and seeds, but for this sauce leave the skins on.

Squab and Rabe

1 tablespoon olive oil
2 squabs, or pigeons, about 1 pound each
Salt and black pepper
4 green onions with tops, chopped fine
1 clove garlic, minced
½ pound broccoli rabe, chopped
2 tablespoons butter
½ cup chicken stock
¼ cup dry vermouth
2 tablespoons Campari

Heat olive oil in a large skillet and brown squabs on both sides, 2 to 3 minutes per side. Season well and add onions, garlic, and broccoli rabe. Brown 2 or 3 minutes more, then lower heat, add butter, chicken stock, vermouth, and Campari, and simmer birds in sauce 15 to 20 minutes, until tender but still rare. Serve hot or at room temperature.

◆ For contrast to the bitterness of the rabe and Campari, accompany the birds with Apricot Sweet Potatoes or Dated Carrots.

◆ If squabs are hard to come by, substitute a pair of quail for each squab. Season and sauté over high heat, then lower heat and sauté until tender, 3 to 4 minutes for split quail, double the time for whole. Remove to a platter and proceed with the other ingredients.

◆ The light bitterness of the rabe and Campari in this preparation might thin out lighter red wines: better to pair it with a medium-bodied Australian or California Cabernet.

Meats

Veal Chops in Brandy Cream
Veal Chops with Pancetta and Goat Cheese
Lemon Veal Scallops
Herbed Veal Breast
Broiled Beef Short Ribs
Beef Fillet Provençal
Beef and Wild Mushroom Sauté
Star-Anise Beef with Snow Peas
Picadillo
Newlywed Meat Loaf
Braised Sweetbreads
Tuscan Liver Sauté
Artichoked Lamb
Dilled Yogurt Lamb
Lamb with Apricots and Almonds
Honey-Mustard Spareribs
Normandy Pork Scallops
Pork in Plum Sauce
Pork Tenderloin with Apricot-Orange Sauce
Venison Steaks
Venison with Mustard Fruits
Rabbit Mole

Veal Chops in Brandy Cream

½ ounce dried porcini mushrooms
1 cup heavy cream
⅛ pound prosciutto
2 veal chops, 1 inch thick
Salt and black pepper
2 tablespoons butter
2 tablespoons olive oil
¼ cup Cognac

Pour 1 cup of boiling water over the mushrooms and soak for 30 minutes. Strain and save the soaking liquid. Rinse the mushrooms, drain, and chop fine. Put the mushrooms in a bowl and add the cream. Strain the mushroom liquid through a doubled paper towel and add to the cream. Shred the prosciutto and add half of it to the cream.

Season the chops with salt and pepper and brown them in a large skillet in the hot oil and butter, about 3 minutes on each side. Add the mushroom cream, cover the skillet, and simmer for 10 to 15 minutes. Remove the chops to a warm platter. Add the Cognac to the sauce and reduce it quickly until the sauce has thickened slightly. Pour the sauce over the chops and sprinkle with the remaining prosciutto.

◆ Serve with a salad of arugula and diced tomatoes.

◆ For simple herbed chops, season the chops, dust them lightly with flour, and press into both sides a mixture of chopped fresh herbs, such as sage, rosemary, and thyme. Brown the chops quickly in the hot butter and oil. Add ¼ cup dry white wine or vermouth, cover, and simmer for 10 minutes or so.

◆ This deserves the best bottle of full-bodied dry white wine you can come up with to match the richness of the mushrooms and the sauce: Meursault or a close equivalent from Burgundy, or else a big Chardonnay from California or Australia.

Veal Chops with Pancetta and Goat Cheese

4 slices pancetta, or prosciutto
2 to 4 slices goat cheese
2 to 3 fresh sage leaves, chopped
1 clove garlic, minced
Salt and black and cayenne peppers
2 loin veal chops (about 1½ pounds), 1 inch thick
Flour
2 tablespoons olive oil
1 tablespoon butter
⅓ cup grated Parmesan cheese

In a large skillet, sauté pancetta 4 or 5 minutes in its own fat until crisp (or sauté prosciutto in a little olive oil). Remove and chop into slivers. Save fat in skillet.

Mix goat cheese with sage, garlic, and seasonings.

Cut each chop in half horizontally to the bone and spread with goat cheese to make a sandwich. Season chops on both sides and dust with flour.

Heat butter and oil in the pancetta skillet and brown chops over high heat, no more than 3 to 4 minutes a side. Sprinkle chops with Parmesan cheese and run under a broiler to brown cheese. Remove to platter and garnish with chopped pancetta.

◆ Serve with grilled (or broiled) fruits or vegetables and end with Banana Zabaglione.

◆ If you prefer scallopine, sauté pancetta as above, then season scallops, dip in flour, and sauté over high heat with chopped sage. For a different sauce, melt goat cheese in pan with a little wine and pour over scallops.

◆ Serve a light Pinot Noir from Oregon or a young Rosso di Montalcino.

Lemon Veal Scallops

1 pound veal scallops
2 lemons
1 cup fresh bread crumbs
½ cup grated Parmesan cheese
Salt and black pepper
1 egg
4 tablespoons butter
2 tablespoons olive oil
1 tablespoon chopped parsley

If the scallops are not ⅛ inch thick, pound them until they are (a rolling pin or heavy jar will do it).

Grate the rind of 1 lemon and mix with the crumbs, cheese, and seasonings. Beat the egg with 2 tablespoons of fresh lemon juice. Dip each scallop in the egg and then in the crumb mixture.

Heat the butter and oil in a large skillet until bubbly. Add the scallops, two or three at a time, and sauté as quickly as possible, about ½ minute on each side. Transfer to a warm platter and keep warm. Add more butter or oil, if needed, until all the scallops are browned.

Add another tablespoon of lemon juice to the pan juices and pour over the scallops. Slice 1 lemon and put the slices over the scallops. Sprinkle with the parsley.

◆ Serve with a butter and cheese pasta and an asparagus vinaigrette.

◆ For traditional veal scallopine, instead of breading the scallops, dust them with seasoned flour and sauté. Add ½ cup heavy cream and ¼ cup Marsala, Madeira, or dry sherry to the pan juices and pour the sauce over the scallops.

◆ The combination of lemon and veal suggests a white with a fair amount of acidity: Sancerre, Premier Cru Chablis, or white Graves. A white Mercurey or Auxey-Duresses from Burgundy would present a softer alternative. For something less expensive, look for a Mâcon-Villages or Italian Chardonnay.

Herbed Veal Breast

1 3-pound veal breast (it's mostly bone)
1½ tablespoons olive oil
2 cloves garlic, minced
2 tablespoons mixed Provençal herbs
Salt and black pepper

Under a broiler, sear the meat on both sides, about 10 minutes a side. Change from the broiler to an oven setting of 400°F.

Mix the olive oil with the garlic, herbs, and seasonings and rub the mixture into the breast on both sides. Cover the top of the breast loosely with aluminum foil and roast for 20 to 30 minutes, until the meat is cooked and the top crisp and well browned.

Cut the top meat diagonally in thin slices and cut between the ribs. The ribs are finger food.

◆ For the country flavors of the Provençal herbs employed here, serve a Merlot that's on the light side—French or California. You can also depend on Pinot Noir to accompany this dish, either Burgundy or American.

Broiled Beef Short Ribs

1 tablespoon Dijon mustard
6 cloves garlic, minced
¼ cup peppercorns, smashed or coarsely ground
Salt
Olive oil
4 to 6 beef short ribs

Make a paste of the mustard, garlic, peppercorns, and salt. Add enough olive oil to make the mixture spreadable. Spread half the paste on the boniest side of the ribs and broil them about 5 minutes. Turn the ribs over, spread on the remaining paste, and broil again for 5 minutes.

Change from the broiler to an oven setting of 425°F. Cover the ribs loosely with aluminum foil and roast another 10 to 15 minutes, until the meat is well browned and tender.

◆ A Bordeaux or California Cabernet will meet the needs of these ribs, as will any well-made, medium-bodied Merlot.

Beef Fillet Provençal

1 pound trimmed beef fillet
1 small onion, finely chopped
1 clove garlic, minced
¼ cup chopped fresh Italian parsley
1 bay leaf, crushed
Salt and black pepper
½ cup red wine
1 tablespoon Cognac
2 tablespoons olive oil
2 to 3 wild mushrooms
¼ cup black Mediterranean olives, pitted and chopped

Marinate the fillet in a mixture of the onion, garlic, parsley, bay leaf, seasonings, wine, and Cognac for 30 minutes (or longer, if you can), turning the meat at least once. Remove the fillet from the marinade and pat it dry. Put it in a roasting pan, baste it with half the olive oil, and roast at 500°F. for 20 minutes, turning the meat after 10 minutes so it roasts evenly. The interior of the meat is done when a meat thermometer registers 120°F. Let the meat rest for 10 minutes before slicing it into ½-inch-thick slices.

While the meat is resting, slice the mushrooms thickly and sauté them in the remaining oil over high heat to brown quickly. Remove the mushrooms from the pan and set aside. To the same pan, add the olives, the marinade, and the juices from the roasting pan and boil for 2 to 3 minutes. For a richer sauce, beat in 2 tablespoons of butter, off the heat. Pour the sauce over the sliced beef and strew the mushrooms over the top.

◆ Serve with Mahogany Potatoes and a mixed vegetable salad. End with a Frozen Chocolate Truffle.

◆ For filet mignon, sauté 2 thick filet steaks over high heat in butter and oil to make them crusty on the outside but rare inside for about

2 to 3 minutes on each side. Remove the steaks and sauté the chopped garlic and wild mushrooms in the same pan. Loosen the pan juices with a splash of Madeira or Cognac and pour the contents of the pan over the steaks.

◆ Bandol would serve as a good traditional match from Provence, but you might also take the opportunity to enjoy a good California Cabernet, its equivalent from Australia or Spain, or one of the sturdier red Bordeaux from Pauillac or St. Estèphe.

Beef and Wild Mushroom Sauté

2 beef fillet steaks, 1¼ inches thick (about ¾ pound total)
Salt and black pepper
2 tablespoons each of butter and olive oil
½ pound wild mushrooms (shiitake, oyster, morel, chanterelle)
2 cloves garlic, minced
2 to 3 sprigs fresh rosemary, or 1 teaspoon dried rosemary

Season fillets and sear in butter and oil in a large skillet, cooking no more than 3 minutes on each side for rare beef. Remove to a warm platter.

Slice mushrooms and add to the skillet, with garlic and rosemary. Sauté over high heat to brown, and scrape onto the steaks.

◆ Serve with Brie-Arugula Salad with Balsamic Cream Dressing and follow with German Fruit Pancake.

◆ Remember Beef Strogonoff? Cut steaks in ¼-inch slices vertically, season, brown very quickly over high heat, and remove to a platter. Sauté mushrooms and add to the meat. Blend 1 teaspoon tomato paste, ½ teaspoon anchovy paste, and a dash of Worcestershire sauce into ⅔ cup sour cream. Mix with beef and mushrooms and return mixture to skillet to warm for a moment or two.

◆ Aged red Burgundy or Bordeaux, especially from the commune of St. Estèphe in the Médoc, are sure bets with this bosky dish.

Star-Anise Beef with Snow Peas

¾ pound beef fillet
2 tablespoons peanut or vegetable oil
1 tablespoon soy sauce
1 whole star-anise, ground
2 or 3 slices gingerroot, minced
1 clove garlic, minced
1 fresh red chili pepper, seeded and minced
1 tablespoon sherry
1 teaspoon sesame oil
½ cup snow peas

Cut beef into slices ¼ inch thick. Place wok over high heat for about 1 minute. Pour in peanut oil, let heat, and add half the beef strips, stir-frying for about 5 seconds. Remove and repeat with remaining strips. Set strips aside.

Mix remaining ingredients, except for snow peas, add to wok, and stir-fry a few seconds. Add snow peas and stir-fry for 1 minute. Remove from heat, add beef, and turn mixture onto serving platter.

◆ Serve with Honeyed Golden Peppers.

◆ Beef strips are delicious with any number of sauces, including the Poblano Sauce (See Charred Shrimp Poblano) or the Green Sauce (See Wok-Smoked Scallops with Green Sauce) or simply a brandied butter with multicolored peppercorns.

◆ For a solid red wine match, try Beaujolais. If you prefer white wine, consider an Alsatian Pinot Gris.

Picadillo

¼ cup currants
2 tablespoons olive oil
1 small onion, chopped fine
1 fresh red or green chili pepper, seeded and minced
2 cloves garlic, minced
½ pound each of ground beef and ground pork
½ cup stuffed green olives, sliced
½ green apple, diced
2 tablespoons tomato purée
1 tablespoon cider vinegar
1 tablespoon capers, drained
1 teaspoon salt
½ teaspoon each of ground cumin and oregano
¼ teaspoon each of ground cinnamon and cloves

Soak currants in hot water to cover for 15 minutes.

Heat oil in a large skillet and sauté onion, pepper, and garlic for 2 to 3 minutes, or until softened. Increase heat, add beef and pork, and lightly brown meats.

Add remaining ingredients, plus currants and their liquid. Cover and simmer for 10 minutes, then remove lid and cook another 5 to 10 minutes to evaporate some of the liquid.

◆ Serve with Parsnip Purée or Pesto Spaghetti Squash.

◆ Make a small molded meat loaf from the same ingredients. Mix sautéed onion, chili pepper, and garlic with raw meats and remaining ingredients, and mix well. Put mixture into a small baking dish and bake at 375°F. for 25 to 30 minutes, or until top is browned.

◆ This happy jumble of sweet and spicy flavors is a fine partner to light, fruity red wines like Beaujolais and Côtes du Rhône.

Newlywed Meat Loaf

1 pound beef chuck, ground
½ pound veal shoulder, ground
½ pound pork shoulder, ground
1 small onion, minced
2 cloves garlic, minced
2 jalapeño peppers, seeded and minced
2 eggs, beaten
1 teaspoon salt
1 teaspoon dried sage
¼ teaspoon black pepper
1 cup tortilla chips, crushed
½ cup dark beer

In a large bowl, mix the meats together with your fingertips. Mix in the onion, garlic, and peppers in the same way. Add the eggs, seasonings, chips, and beer and mix until well blended. The texture should be light and moist.

Pack the mixture into a standard loaf pan, cover the top tightly with aluminum foil, and bake at 350°F. for 1 to 1¼ hours. Remove the foil for the final 20 minutes to brown the top and evaporate excess liquid.

◆ The beef-veal-pork combination suggests a rustic companion: maybe something a little out of the way, such as a wine from the Provence region of France—a Bandol Rouge, or perhaps a Côtes du Ventoux, wines with pronounced earthy flavors.

Braised Sweetbreads

3 green onions with tops
1 carrot
1 stalk celery
1 sweet red pepper
1 tablespoon butter
1 tablespoon olive oil
1 pair sweetbreads
Salt and black pepper
1 cup dry white wine
2 teaspoons Dijon mustard
1 teaspoon balsamic vinegar

Finely chop all the vegetables and in a medium skillet sauté them until lightly browned in the butter and oil. Lay the sweetbreads on top, season well, and pour in the wine. Cook, covered, over low heat for 30 minutes. Remove the sweetbreads to a plate, put a board or a plate on top and weight with a can to press the sweetbreads slightly.

Purée the vegetables in a processor or blender. If the sweetbreads have not been trimmed, remove the outside membranes and connecting tubes. Add the trimmings to the processor. Add the mustard and vinegar and process again. Taste for seasoning. Cut the sweetbreads crosswise into 1-inch-thick slices. Reheat briefly in the skillet with the puréed sauce.

◆ Serve with a crisp green salad and baked chèvre (herbed and oiled, and baked at 350°F. for 10 minutes).

◆ For broiled sweetbreads: If the sweetbreads are not trimmed, parboil them gently in simmering water with a little salt and fresh lemon juice for 15 minutes. Drain and run under cold water. Trim off the membranes and tubes and discard. Spread the sweetbreads with Dijon mustard and roll them in bread crumbs mixed with chopped fresh herbs. Broil or sauté until the crumbs are well browned on all sides.

◆ The delicacy of the sweetbreads suggests either a medium-bodied red Bordeaux from Margaux or St. Julien or a similar red Burgundy (try Fixin or Savigny). Red Rioja is another attractive possibility.

Tuscan Liver Sauté

1 pound calves' liver, thinly sliced
Salt and black pepper
2 tablespoons olive oil
1 tablespoon butter
1 red onion, sliced very thin
1 clove garlic, minced
1 tablespoon chopped fresh sage
Lemon wedges or balsamic vinegar

Cut off any membranes and, if the liver pieces are thicker than ¼ inch, cut them horizontally to make thinner slices. Season and cut liver into 1-inch strips.

In a large skillet, heat oil and butter and sauté onion, garlic, and sage for 1 or 2 minutes to soften them. Over high heat, add liver and brown quickly, about 1 minute total, to avoid toughening. Serve with lemon wedges or sprinkle with balsamic vinegar.

◆ Chinese Cabbage and Pink Grapefruit Slaw makes a good contrast of flavor and texture.

◆ A slight variation is to sauté the liver in larger pieces and to sprinkle with Italian *gremolata*, or equal parts chopped parsley, garlic, and lemon rind.

◆ Liver can be tough on many wines, but this simple preparation is delicious next to light, red Burgundies like Santenay and Mercurey.

Artichoked Lamb

2 tablespoons olive oil
2 loin lamb chops, 1 ½ inches thick
4 cooked artichoke hearts, quartered
2 Belgian endives, halved
6 garlic cloves, halved
12 Mediterranean olives, green or black
1 teaspoon mixed dried herbs, such as sage, rosemary, thyme, and oregano
Salt and black pepper

Heat the olive oil in a large skillet over high heat and sear the lamb chops quickly on both sides. Arrange the chops with the vegetables, garlic, and olives in a baking dish, sprinkle them with the herbs and seasonings, and pour the pan juices over the whole. Cover the dish with aluminum foil and seal the edges tightly. Bake at 325°F. for 15 or 20 minutes for rare to medium-rare lamb.

◆ Serve with crusty French bread to absorb the garlic and juices. End with Margarita Oranges.

◆ To make a Lamb Ratatouille, sear the chops as above, but instead of endive and artichoke hearts, add cubed eggplant, zucchini, fresh tomatoes, and minced onion to the skillet with the garlic and herbs. Cover and cook over low heat for 10 to 15 minutes.

◆ Lamb is the traditional match for a good red Bordeaux from the Médoc. The artichokes, however, change things slightly, suggesting the less austere qualities of a Pomerol or a good California Merlot. If you like a strong red, try a northern Rhône, such as Cornas or Saint Joseph, or wines made elsewhere from the same grape: California Syrah or Australian Shiraz.

Dilled Yogurt Lamb

2 large loin lamb chops (about 1½ pounds), cut thick
Salt and black pepper
2 tablespoons olive oil
1 red onion, sliced
4 cloves garlic, chopped
1 cup plain yogurt
2 tablespoons crumbled feta cheese
3 tablespoons chopped fresh dill
1 tablespoon chopped fresh cilantro

In a large skillet, season lamb and sear it on all sides in the oil. Remove chops and set aside.

In the same pan, sauté onion and garlic 3 to 4 minutes, or until softened. Remove pan from the heat and stir in yogurt, cheese, and half the fresh herbs.

Return chops to pan, cover, and simmer over very low heat about 10 to 15 minutes, or until meat is tender. Remove chops to platter, pour sauce over them, and garnish with remaining herbs.

◆ Serve with Green Rice.

◆ A dilled yogurt sauce is also fine for a lamb loin, pan-grilled or broiled to keep it rare. Purée the sautéed onion and garlic with ½ cup yogurt, 4 tablespoons feta cheese, and ½ tablespoon balsamic vinegar.

◆ Here's a lamb chop that goes nicely—because the lamb is not rare—with white wine. Try it with a full-bodied California Chardonnay or a white Burgundy such as Meursault.

Lamb with Apricots and Almonds

1 tablespoon olive oil
1- to 1½-pound-piece boneless lamb, from loin
1 teaspoon black pepper
Salt to taste
½ small onion, minced
½ teaspoon each *of ground cumin and coriander*
¼ teaspoon ground cinnamon
4 to 6 dried apricots, soaked in ½ cup boiling water
¼ cup red wine
2 tablespoons almonds, toasted and ground

Put oil in a large skillet. Roll lamb in the oil, season meat with pepper and salt. Remove meat and heat skillet until it begins to smoke. Brown lamb well on all sides and, when it is tender, remove to a warm serving platter.

In same skillet, sauté onion with spices.

Purée apricots with their liquid and wine in a blender and add to skillet. Scrape in any meat juices and heat through. If sauce is too thick, add a little boiling water.

Slice lamb diagonally, pour sauce over it, and sprinkle with toasted almonds.

◆ Serve with Turnip-Pear Purée or Braised Onions and Lemons.

◆ For a luxury dish, serve the seared lamb in a reduced red wine sauce, similarly spiced and garnished with fresh sliced figs.

◆ Here's another meat dish that is improved more by a white wine than a red wine. The apricot's balance of acid and sweet is a perfect set-up for a Gewürztraminer from Alsace or California.

Honey–Mustard Spareribs

1 side lean spareribs (about 2 pounds)
¼ cup honey
¼ cup Dijon mustard
2 teaspoons soy sauce
2 tablespoons cider vinegar
2 cloves garlic, peeled and mashed
1 fresh red or green chili pepper, or Tabasco sauce to taste
3 cups sauerkraut, rinsed and drained
1 medium onion, diced
1 cup dry white wine

Trim off excess fat and make a shallow cut between each rib. Drop ribs into a large pot of boiling water and simmer for 40 minutes. Drain well.

Make basting sauce of honey, mustard, soy sauce, vinegar, garlic, and chili by mixing in a blender.

Place sauerkraut, onion, and wine in a shallow baking dish. Lay ribs on top and brush on both sides with sauce, placing ribs fat-side up. Roast at 400°F. for 20 minutes, basting until all sauce is used.

To serve, cut between every rib, or every two ribs, and place sauerkraut to the side.

◆ Good with Roasted Potato Chips.

◆ If you have enough time, roast the ribs, without poaching, at 375°F. for about 1½ hours. Cover ribs with basting sauce and cover pan with aluminum foil. Bake 50 minutes with foil on, add sauerkraut, and continue baking ribs uncovered for 30 to 40 minutes more, or until browned.

◆ Simple, fruity reds like young Zinfandels and Barberas are great with sweet and sour ribs.

Normandy Pork Scallops

1 pound pork scallops
Salt and black pepper
Flour
1 tablespoon olive oil
4 tablespoons butter
2 tart green apples
1 small onion, sliced
2 tablespoons Calvados

Pound the scallops, if needed, to make them ¼-inch thick. Season, dredge with the flour, and brown quickly on both sides (1 to 2 minutes on each side) in a large skillet in the oil and butter. Remove the pork and set aside.

Quarter the apples, core and peel them, and slice them ½-inch thick. Sauté the onion and apples in the hot butter until they are lightly browned. Add the Calvados and the pork, cover the skillet, and simmer for 3 to 4 minutes, or until the pork is just cooked through but not dried out.

◆ Pork is always good with noodles or potatoes. End with a plum tart.

◆ Do a Chinese pork stir-fry. Brown the pork scallops quickly in 2 tablespoons of peanut oil. Add minced hot pepper, gingerroot, garlic, and green onions, and fry for 1 minute. Add 1 tablespoon soy sauce, 2 tablespoons dry sherry, and 1 teaspoon white wine vinegar. Cook for 1 minute and transfer to a platter. Sprinkle the pork with toasted sesame seeds.

◆ Red and white are equally good here. The apples will be best matched by a California Riesling or Mosel Kabinett. For a red, try Merlot or Cabernet from Long Island, Italian Merlot, or else a Chinon or Bourgueil from the Loire.

Pork in Plum Sauce

1 pound pork tenderloin
Salt and black pepper
1 tablespoon olive oil
4 red-skinned plums, such as Santa Clara
1 cup hearty red wine, such as Burgundy
½ teaspoon ground cardamom
¼ teaspoon ground cinnamon
⅛ teaspoon ground cloves

Heat a heavy skillet; season pork and brown it well on all sides in oil, for about 10 minutes (or roast at 450°F. for 10 to 15 minutes). Remove to a warm platter.

Halve plums, remove pits, and quarter each half. Add plums, wine, and seasonings to skillet, cover, and simmer over low heat for 10 to 15 minutes, or until tender.

Slice pork crosswise and garnish with half the plums. Put remaining plums in a blender with the liquid and purée. Pour sauce over pork and plums.

◆ Excellent with Garlic Roast Potatoes or Honeyed Golden Peppers.

◆ Make a similar sauce with prunes and brandy. Soak ½ cup prunes in boiling water. Simmer the prunes in their liquid with the seasonings, and add ¼ cup brandy for the final 3 or 4 minutes.

◆ This dish practically begs for a young, fruity Pinot Noir from Oregon or from a cooler part of California.

Pork Tenderloin with Apricot–Orange Sauce

1- to 1½-pounds pork tenderloin

MARINADE:
¼ cup olive oil
2 cloves garlic, minced
3 slices fresh ginger, minced
¼ cup mixed fresh chopped herbs, such as rosemary, thyme, chives, mint, sage
1 teaspoon balsamic vinegar
Salt and black and cayenne peppers

FOR THE SAUCE:
8 dried apricots, chopped
⅔ cup fresh orange juice
¼ teaspoon black pepper
½ teaspoon soy sauce

Put the pork in a zip-seal plastic bag with the mixed ingredients of the marinade and refrigerate for 24 hours. Massage the meat in the bag from time to time to make sure all sides are well coated.

Either charcoal-grill the loin over hot embers, for about 7 to 10 minutes (turning frequently), or roast it in a 450°F. oven for 10 to 20 minutes. Let it rest a few minutes before slicing.

Meanwhile, make the sauce. In a blender purée the apricots, the remaining ingredients, and any meat drippings or juices from the roast. Slice the roast and serve the sauce separately.

◆ The sturdiness of this dish—ginger, the mixed herbs, the balsamic vinegar—suggests one of the many excellent California Zinfandels, such as those made by Ravenswood, Grgich Hills, and Peachy Canyon. Or, to take a different tack, drink one of the newish California varietals, such as Barbera or Sangiovese.

Venison Steaks

1 pound venison steaks, 1½ inches thick
Salt and coarsely ground black pepper
2 tablespoons butter
2 tablespoons olive oil
1 small fresh chili pepper, minced
1 tablespoon tomato paste
1 tablespoon cranberry preserves or currant jelly
1 tablespoon red wine vinegar
2 tablespoons Port or Madeira
½ cup red wine
Dash of Worcestershire sauce

Season the steaks well on both sides. Heat the butter and oil in a large heavy skillet and sear the steaks on both sides, 5 to 7 minutes on each side for rare meat. Transfer the steaks to a hot platter and make the game sauce by stirring the remaining ingredients into the pan juices. Bring to a boil, taste for sweet and sour, and adjust by adding more cranberry preserves or vinegar. Pour the sauce over the steaks.

◆ Serve with a good winter vegetable, such as puréed turnips, and end with Maple Toffee Apples or Pears.

◆ For broiled steaks, season the steaks and coat them with oil. Broil close to the flame, 4 minutes on each side. Top each steak with a large spoonful of herb butter (mix 4 tablespoons softened butter with chopped parsley and garlic, or chopped basil, thyme, rosemary, mint, oregano—whatever you can get fresh).

◆ The richness of game calls for the strongest reds of all: full-bodied Cabernets or Zinfandels from California (Ridge Vineyards is an excellent source for both varieties), a Hermitage, Côte Rôtie, or good Château-neuf-du-Pape from the Rhône, or a good Barolo or Barbaresco from Italy. Red Bordeaux from the northern Médoc (Pauillac or St. Estèphe) would also make an excellent match.

Venison with Mustard Fruits

4 venison noisettes (from the loin), about 1 pound
Salt and black and cayenne peppers
2 tablespoons olive oil
⅓ cup currant jelly
2 tablespoons Dijon mustard
1 cup blueberries or blackberries

Season steaks and sauté in oil in large hot skillet 3 to 4 minutes on each side. Remove to a warm platter.

Melt jelly in the same skillet with mustard. Add fruit and simmer just enough to warm it. Pour over venison.

◆ Serve with Zucchini Gratin and end with Oatmeal-Nut Shortbread and your favorite ice cream.

◆ For a Southern touch, flame the seared noisettes in ¼ cup warmed bourbon and serve with pickled watermelon rind or peach chutney.

◆ Sturdy young red wines bursting with berry fruit are splendid accompaniments to venison. Try a Châteauneuf-du-Pape or a full-bodied California Syrah.

Rabbit Mole

1 2- to 3-pound fresh rabbit, cut into pieces
Flour
Salt, and black pepper
¼ cup olive oil
1 small onion, chopped
2 cloves garlic, mashed
¼ cup pumpkin seeds
2 tablespoons sunflower seeds
¼ teaspoon cumin seeds
1 dried red chili pepper, crumbled
3 sprigs fresh coriander
1 cup chicken stock
1 tablespoon grated bitter chocolate

Dust the rabbit pieces with seasoned flour. Heat the oil in a large heavy skillet and brown the pieces on both sides. Remove the rabbit and in the same pan sauté the onion, garlic, seeds, and chili pepper for 5 minutes. Put in a blender with the coriander, stock, and chocolate and purée. Taste for seasoning and adjust, making it spicier with more chili or blander with more pumpkin seeds. Return the rabbit to the skillet, pour the sauce over it, cover, and simmer for 20 to 30 minutes.

◆ Serve with a salad of arugula and oranges. End with guava paste and mascarpone served on crisp crackers.

◆ Stuff a whole rabbit with fresh bread crumbs mixed with chopped and sautéed mushrooms, garlic, and the rabbit liver if available. Season well. Coat the rabbit with oil and roast at 400°F. for 50 to 60 minutes. Melt 4 tablespoons butter and baste the rabbit while it is roasting. When the rabbit is done, sauté ¼ pound wild mushrooms and 1 clove minced garlic in the basting butter and use as a sauce.

◆ Certain red wines have a "chocolaty" quality that goes well with mole: try a medium-bodied Zinfandel, a Nebbiolo d'Alba, or a sturdy Rhône red such as Gigondas.

Afterward

Margarita Oranges
Chili Oranges
Blackened Figs
Gingered Figs
Hot Mint-Julep Peaches
Sautéed Peaches and Cream
Maple Toffee Apples or Pears
Avocado-Pineapple Cream
Fresh Fruit Macedonia
Papaya-Tomato Compote
Pernod Pears
Dried Apricot Fool
Apricot Crepes
Walnut-Apricot Tart
Plum Mascarpone Tart with Quick Nut Crust
German Fruit Pancake
Feather Pancakes with Blueberry Sauce
Raspberry Ricotta and Cream
Banana Zabaglione
Mango-Chili Cream
Ice Cream with White-Chocolate Raspberry Sauce
Jalapeño-Lime Ice
Grape Freezies
Chocolate-Chili Cream
Frozen Chocolate Truffle
Brandy Alexander Parfait
Mandarin Sorbet

Oatmeal-Nut Shortbread
Fresh Gingercake
Sicilian Biscotti
Orange-Almond Balls
Hazelnut Chocolate Wafers
Black Chocolate Polenta

Margarita Oranges

2 navel oranges
2 tablespoons powdered sugar
Juice of 2 limes
2 tablespoons Tequila
1½ tablespoons Cointreau or Triple Sec

Peel the oranges and section them. Sprinkle with the sugar, lime juice, Tequila, and Cointreau, cover with plastic wrap, and refrigerate until ready to serve.

◆ For another option you can macerate the peeled and sliced oranges in rose water or fresh orange juice and sprinkle them with cinnamon.

◆ Any good sweet muscat is the perfect complement to oranges: Muscat Beaumes de Venise from the Rhône, California Muscat (try Quady's "Essencia"), or an Italian Moscato.

Chili Oranges

2 navel (or blood) oranges
1 teaspoon pure ground chili (mild)
¼ teaspoon salt
Fresh cilantro sprigs for garnish

Peel oranges, remove pith, and slice thin.

Mix chili and salt and sprinkle mixture over oranges. Garnish with cilantro sprigs.

◆ A real palate cleanser at the end of a rich meal.

◆ Try the orange-chili combination in a sorbet, puréeing orange pulp with extra orange juice, adding a sugar syrup (or orange marmalade) to chili, and freezing.

◆ Try a wine made from orange muscat, such as Essencia.

Blackened Figs

½ pound dried figs
3 cups red wine
½ cup honey
½ cup Port

Put figs in a deep baking dish and cover with the red wine and honey. Bake at 350°F. for 1 hour. (The figs will absorb most of the liquid and turn almost black in color.) Pour the Port over the figs and stir to dissolve the remaining liquid. Serve by themselves or with vanilla ice cream.

◆ If the figs are served alone, try a California Muscat, Italian Moscato, or Muscat Beaumes de Venise.

Gingered Figs

1 cup dried figs
¼ cup candied ginger, chopped
2 tablespoons sugar
Juice of ½ lemon
1 cup boiling water
¼ cup walnuts, chopped

Put figs in a small saucepan with ginger. Mix sugar, lemon juice, and water and pour over figs. Cover pan and simmer gently for 20 to 30 minutes until figs are plump and tender. Put figs in a bowl, sprinkle with nuts, and serve warm or chilled.

◆ Think of this as a fruit dessert with a little extra zing.

◆ Try a mixture of chopped figs, dates, and prunes, simmered the same way, and served with yogurt mixed with nuts and honey.

◆ Late-harvest Gewürztraminers from California are fine accompaniments to simple fig-based desserts.

Hot Mint-Julep Peaches

2 ripe peaches
1 tablespoon butter
1 tablespoon sugar
2 tablespoons bourbon
¼ cup chopped fresh mint leaves

Peel and slice peaches. Heat butter until bubbly in a medium skillet over high heat. Add peaches and remaining ingredients. Turn fruit gently just to warm it through. Serve hot or at room temperature.

◆ This is a fine summer dessert to serve cold, but if you chill it, add another tablespoon of sugar with a teaspoon of lime juice to prevent peaches from turning brown.

◆ Flavor your peaches this way when making a peach shortcake, covered with whipped cream.

◆ A festive ending to a meal, especially when served with a light sparkling Moscato d'Asti.

Sautéed Peaches and Cream

1 tablespoon butter
2 to 3 ripe peaches, peeled and sliced
1 tablespoon brown sugar
½ to ⅔ cup heavy cream

Heat the butter in a skillet until sizzling, add the peach slices, and sprinkle them with sugar. Quickly turn them over in the butter and add the cream. Heat to a simmer and serve immediately.

Maple Toffee Apples or Pears

2 firm apples or pears
2 tablespoons fresh lemon juice
3 tablespoons butter
2 tablespoons brown sugar
¼ cup maple syrup
¼ cup heavy cream
1 teaspoon vanilla extract
⅓ cup toasted chopped pecans

Quarter, core, peel, and slice the apples or pears. Place in a medium bowl and sprinkle them with the lemon juice.

Make a sauce by melting 1 tablespoon of the butter with the brown sugar, maple syrup, and cream in a small saucepan. Boil the sauce, stirring, for 4 to 5 minutes, or until it thickens. Remove from the heat and add the vanilla.

In a medium heavy skillet, fry the fruit slices in the remaining butter over high heat to cook them slightly but not until they are limp. Pour the sauce over them and sprinkle with the pecans.

◆An Auslese from the Mosel will match both the richness of the sauce and the particular flavors of pears and apples. Sauternes would also be appropriate.

Avocado–Pineapple Cream

1 ripe avocado
1 lime
½ fresh pineapple
2 to 3 tablespoons honey
2 tablespoons Kirsch or other fruit brandy

Cut the avocado into quarters, peel, and put the flesh into a processor or blender. Grate the rind of the lime and add it to the avocado with the juice of the lime.

Cut the pineapple half in two, lengthwise. Remove the center core and slice the flesh crosswise; then cut the flesh from the rind as if cutting off a melon rind. Add the pineapple slices, honey, and Kirsch to the avocado and purée until smooth. Taste and add more lime or honey accordingly.

Scoop the purée into a metal pan (to conduct cold) and put in the freezer until ready to serve. If the cream is frozen hard, spoon it into a processor and whip it again into a purée; then serve.

◆ Avocado is not a suitable match for most wines, but a sparkling dessert wine, such as a Champagne Doux or an Asti Spumante, would do fine.

Fresh Fruit Macedonia

1 cup each *of strawberries, cherries, plums, red grapes, and blueberries*
1 lemon
2 tablespoons honey
1 tablespoon Crème de Cassis
½ cup Port
¼ teaspoon ground cinnamon
¼ cup shelled pistachios

Hull the strawberries, pit the cherries, and stone the plums, cutting them into quarters if they are large. If the grapes have seeds, cut the grapes in half and remove the seeds. Grate the lemon rind and mix with the honey, Cassis, Port, and cinnamon.

Put the fruit in a serving bowl, pour the liquid over it, cover with plastic wrap, and refrigerate until ready to serve. Sprinkle the pistachios over the top before serving.

◆ An Alsatian Gewürztraminer Vendange Tardive will provide the right balance between sweetness and spice, though a Tawny Port or Banyuls could be enjoyed as well.

Papaya–Tomato Compote

½ small red papaya
4 to 5 plum tomatoes, quartered
1 lime
¼ cup sugar, or to taste
⅓ cup fresh pineapple juice

Cube the papaya in bite-size chunks and seed the quartered tomatoes. Combine the fruit in a small saucepan, add the zest of the lime, the juice of half the lime, and the sugar and pineapple juice. Bring the mixture to the simmer and taste for the balance of sweet and tart. Add more lime juice or more sugar as wanted. Simmer gently until the tomatoes yield their juice but the fruit is still firm. Serve warm or cold.

Pernod Pears

2 ripe pears
2 tablespoons unsalted pistachio nuts, chopped coarsely
2 tablespoons Pernod

Halve pears, peel, remove core, and place pears cavity-side up on a square of aluminum foil. Fill each cavity with nuts and pour Pernod over top. Bring foil up around pears and seal edges tightly. Bake at 400°F. for 30 minutes. Serve hot, warm, or cold.

◆ Refreshingly light after a hearty meal.

◆ Instead of pistachios, fill the cavities with candied ginger and use Kirsch or, if you're feeling extravagant, the pear brandy called Poire.

◆ Delicious next to a glass of late-harvest California or Australian Riesling.

Dried Apricot Fool

½ cup dried apricots
1 to 2 tablespoons fresh lemon juice
2 tablespoons apricot jam
1 tablespoon almond liqueur (see Note below)
½ cup heavy cream, whipped

Cover apricots with water in a small saucepan, bring to a boil, and simmer for 10 minutes. Drain but reserve liquid.

Purée apricots in a food processor with lemon juice, jam, and liqueur. If more liquid is needed, add enough apricot liquid to make a thick purée.

Whip cream and fold into fruit mixture. Pile mixture into glass bowls.

◆ Serve with Oatmeal-Nut Shortbread.

◆ Turn mixture into a frozen soufflé by beating 2 egg whites until foamy, then gradually adding ¼ cup confectioners' sugar and continuing to beat until whites are stiff but not dry. Fold in the apricot purée with its flavorings and the whipped cream, turn it into a mold, and freeze.

Note: You can substitute ½ teaspoon almond flavoring, plus 1 teaspoon or more Kirsch.

Apricot Crepes

CREPE BATTER:
½ *cup milk*
1 *tablespoon butter*
1 *tablespoon sugar*
Zest from 1 orange
¼ *cup fresh orange juice*
¼ *cup flour*
¼ *cup corn flour, or very finely ground cornmeal*
Pinch of salt
1 *egg*

FILLING:
1 *cup crème fraîche*
½ *cup apricot preserves*
3 *tablespoons Grand Marnier*
Confectioners' sugar

In a small saucepan, bring the milk to the simmer with the butter and sugar. Pour the mixture into a blender and add the remaining ingredients for the batter. Blend until smooth.

Grease a small crepe pan or skillet and heat it until a drop of water sizzles. Ladle about ¼ cup of the batter onto the pan and swirl it around to reach the edges. Brown it quickly on both sides. Repeat with the remaining batter.

Mix the crème fraîche, apricot preserves, and liqueur together. Spoon one quarter of the mixture onto each crepe and roll them up. Sprinkle with confectioners' sugar.

Makes about 4 crepes.

Walnut–Apricot Tart

1 cup dried apricots, chopped
⅓ cup dark rum
¾ cup walnuts
¾ cup flour
¾ cup brown sugar
6 tablespoons butter, melted
3 eggs, beaten
¼ cup honey
1 teaspoon vanilla extract
Ground cinnamon and whipped cream

Soak the apricots in the rum while making the crust. Coarsely grind the walnuts in a processor and mix half of them with the flour, sugar, and butter. Press the mixture onto the bottom and sides of a 9-inch pie pan. Sprinkle with the remaining walnuts.

Beat together the apricot mixture, eggs, honey, and vanilla. Pour the mixture into the crust and bake at 350°F. for 30 to 40 minutes, or until the eggs are set. Sprinkle with cinnamon and serve with whipped cream.

◆ California late-harvest Rieslings are good with apricots, but Sauternes, Rhine Auslese, or an Alsatian Vendange Tardive would also work well.

Plum Mascarpone Tart with Quick Nut Crust

CRUST:
2 cups walnuts
2 tablespoons brown sugar
1 egg white, beaten

FILLING:
1 pound Italian purple plums
½ cup plum jam or blueberry preserves
Rind and juice of 1 lemon
¼ cup Port wine
⅓ cup hazelnuts, toasted and ground
½ pound mascarpone
½ cup sour cream

To make crust, toast walnuts for about 8 to 10 minutes over low heat in skillet, then grind nuts in food processor. Mix with sugar and beat in egg white. Press mixture evenly into a 9-inch pie pan and bake at 300°F. for 15 to 20 minutes, until lightly browned.

Remove pits from plums and put plums in food processor with jam, lemon, and Port. Pulse several times to make a chunky purée. Taste for sweetness and add more jam if desired.

Sprinkle half the hazelnuts over the baked crust and spoon in the purée to make an even layer. Beat mascarpone with sour cream and cover plums with white swirls. Sprinkle top with remaining nuts.

A very showy conclusion to a grand or simple meal.

◆ Almost any fresh fruits can be treated this way, according to the season. Think of chunked peaches with peach jam, apricots with apricot jam, strawberries with strawberry jam, etc.

◆ Try a late-harvest Zinfandel or young Ruby Port.

German Fruit Pancake

2 eggs
½ cup milk
½ cup flour
1 teaspoon sugar
⅛ teaspoon salt
3 tablespoons butter
½ cup orange marmalade

Put eggs, milk, flour, sugar, and salt in a blender and blend until smooth.

Melt butter in an 8-inch-wide heavy skillet in oven heated to 425°F. When skillet is hot, pour in batter and return pan to oven. Bake for 10 to 15 minutes, until pancake is puffed and browned.

Spread pancake with marmalade, cut it into quarters, and serve like a pizza.

◆ This is a lazy man's popover to cover with any kind of jam.

◆ Turn a German pancake into a French *clafouti* by pouring batter over 2 cups chopped fresh fruit, such as apples, peaches, or berries mixed with fruit preserves. Bake in a hot skillet as above.

Feather Pancakes with Blueberry Sauce

2 eggs
⅔ cup sour cream
4 tablespoons butter, melted
6 tablespoons flour
2 teaspoons sugar
⅛ teaspoon salt

Put all the ingredients into a blender and blend until smooth. Heat a griddle, crepe pan, or heavy skillet, grease it with butter and when hot, ladle on the batter to make small pancakes (these will be light as crepes but not as thin). Serve with maple or birch syrup, melted currant jelly or orange marmalade, or Blueberry Sauce.

◆ Good for a meal, as well as dessert.

Blueberry Sauce

1 pint fresh blueberries
¼ cup maple syrup
¼ cup water
1 teaspoon vanilla extract

Put 1 cup of the blueberries into a blender with the other ingredients and blend until smooth. Heat the mixture in a small saucepan until it simmers. Add the remaining cup of blueberries and return to the simmer, then remove from the heat.

Raspberry Ricotta and Cream

1 cup fresh whole-milk ricotta cheese
½ to 1 pint fresh raspberries
1 teaspoon cinnamon
¼ cup sugar
½ cup mascarpone, or heavy cream whipped lightly

Put the ricotta cheese in a glass bowl and cover it with the raspberries. Sprinkle the cinnamon and sugar over the raspberries and top with mascarpone cheese or whipped cream.

Banana Zabaglione

3 egg yolks
3 tablespoons sugar
⅓ cup Marsala
1 banana
1 teaspoon fresh lemon juice
2 amaretti biscuits, crushed, for garnish

Mix egg yolks with sugar and beat with a whisk or an electric egg beater in top part of double boiler, over boiling water. When mixture becomes light and fluffy, add Marsala a little at a time and beat strenuously until all is absorbed.

Slice banana, divide slices between two glass bowls, and sprinkle lemon juice over slices. Pour zabaglione over bananas and sprinkle with crushed amaretti. Serve hot or cold.

◆ A good Italianate ending to a dinner of pasta and salad.

◆ Great with a chilled glass of Marsala, or whatever sweet wine is used in the preparation.

◆ Instead of Marsala, beat in another sweet dessert wine such as Essencia (made of orange muscat grapes), Tokay, or Sauternes, and serve over sliced peaches or nectarines.

Mango-Chili Cream

2 small or 1 large ripe mango, peeled and sliced
Zest and juice of 1 lime
1 to 2 teaspoons pure ground chili (medium hot)
⅔ cup heavy cream

Purée mango slices with 2 teaspoons of the lime juice, 1 teaspoon ground chili, and the cream. Taste and add additional lime juice or chili as needed. Blend in the lime zest and divide the mixture into two parfait or sorbet glasses. Chill for at least an hour before serving.

Ice Cream with White-Chocolate Raspberry Sauce

1 pint fresh raspberries
¼ pound white chocolate
½ cup heavy cream
¼ cup honey
¾ pint vanilla ice cream

Purée raspberries in blender and sieve to remove seeds.

Melt chocolate with heavy cream and honey over low heat, stirring until chocolate dissolves. Simmer mixture until it thickens slightly, 2 or 3 minutes. Remove from heat and let cool for 5 minutes.

Pour chocolate sauce and raspberry purée in swirls over ice cream.

◆ Not for every day, maybe, but on the other hand, why not?

◆ Use the same sauce to cover fresh fruit or to cloak a meringue glacé.

Jalapeño–Lime Ice

1 cup sugar
3 jalapeño peppers, seeded and minced
1½ cups water
Rind and juice of 2 to 3 limes (½ cup juice)

Put sugar and peppers in a small saucepan with the water and heat, stirring, until sugar is dissolved. Cool quickly in the refrigerator. Add lime, taste thoroughly for the exact degree of sweet, sour, and hot that you want, remembering that freezing will diminish flavor. Freeze mixture in metal tray or bowl.

◆ This makes a refreshing ice between courses, as well as a dessert.

◆ Use orange juice instead of lime, substituting 2 cups juice and pulp (free of membranes), plus orange rind.

Grape Freezies

1 bunch red seedless grapes
½ cup confectioners' sugar

Put grapes in freezer for about 30 minutes. Take out, sift sugar over them, and serve. The grapes should be very cold but not frozen.

For a pretty dessert centerpiece, surround grapes with slices of Chinese star-fruit, sometimes called carombola, dipped in sugar.

◆ For a grape ice, purée fresh red seedless grapes in a blender with grape juice, lemon juice, and sugar syrup. Freeze as quickly as possible.

Chocolate–Chili Cream

2 ounces high-quality bittersweet chocolate
2 tablespoons espresso coffee, brewed very strong
¼ cup heavy cream
1 teaspoon pure ground chili
2 tablespoons skinned hazelnuts, chopped

Melt chocolate slowly with coffee, cream, and chili over a very low flame, stirring as needed. Simmer to thicken slightly, about 10 minutes.

Pour mixture into 2 small pots-de-crème cups or small bowls and chill for at least 30 minutes. Sprinkle tops with the hazelnuts.

◆ Serve instead of chocolate truffles with coffee after a meal of splendor.

◆ Mexico has put chocolate, coffee, and chili together for a couple of thousand years and the combination does wonders for cookies and cakes as well as sauces. For a sauce, mix proportions above with 1 cup crème fraîche and cover with fresh raspberries.

Frozen Chocolate Truffle

3 ounces high-quality bittersweet chocolate
1 tablespoon strong espresso coffee
6 tablespoons butter, cut into 6 slices
2 tablespoons Cognac or Grand Marnier
2 eggs, separated
2 tablespoons superfine sugar
¼ cup hazelnuts, toasted and finely chopped

Melt the chocolate with the coffee in the top of a double boiler over simmering water. Beat in the butter, remove from the heat, and add the Cognac.

In a medium bowl, beat the egg yolks with the sugar until thick. In a medium bowl, beat the egg whites until stiff but not dry.

Beat the chocolate mixture into the egg yolks. Fold in the whites, sprinkle the top with the nuts, and put in the freezer until ready to serve.

◆ There *is* a wine that can be happily consumed with chocolate: California Port (look for Quady or Ficklin) or, better yet, a late-harvest Zinfandel.

Brandy Alexander Parfait

¾ pint vanilla ice cream
3 tablespoons crème de cacao
3 tablespoons brandy
¼ cup heavy cream
¼ cup hazelnuts, toasted and ground

Scoop ice cream into 2 parfait glasses. Pour crème de cacao, brandy, and cream into blender and whip until slightly thickened. Pour mixture over ice cream and top with toasted hazelnuts.

◆ Good for when you want a little something extra.

◆ Make a delicious frozen Brandy Alexander. Chop up the hazelnuts in a food processor. Then add the rest of the ingredients and purée. Freeze the mixture, puréeing it quickly again just before serving.

Mandarin Sorbet

1 11-ounce can of mandarin oranges in syrup
½ teaspoon almond extract
2 tablespoons Grand Marnier

Put the can of mandarins in the freezer until solidly frozen. Submerge the can in a pot of hot water for a minute. Then remove the lid and slip the contents, including all liquid, into a food processor. Pulse to chop up the solids. Add the almond extract and liqueur and process until smooth. Serve immediately.

Oatmeal-Nut Shortbread

¼ pound butter
⅓ cup brown sugar
½ cup flour
⅛ teaspoon salt
⅓ cup rolled oats
½ teaspoon vanilla extract
½ cup walnuts or pecans, chopped
Ground cinnamon and granulated sugar for the top

Cream butter and sugar until fluffy, or pulse in food processor until smooth. Mix flour, salt, oats, and vanilla and mix lightly with butter-sugar mixture, or pulse in processor until just mixed (as in making pastry dough). Add nuts and mix well.

Press dough with your fingertips into an 8- or 9-inch pie pan, and with a sharp knife mark top into 8 or 12 pieces. Sprinkle top with cinnamon and granulated sugar. Bake at 300°F. for about 25 minutes, until lightly browned. Cut pieces all the way through and let cool in pan.

◆ A nice companion for fruit sherbets or fresh fruit and an essential for afternoon tea.

◆ For a savory instead of a sweet shortbread, omit sugar and vanilla and mix butter, flour, oats, and nuts with salt, cumin, lots of black pepper, and ¼ cup grated cheddar cheese.

Fresh Gingercake

¾ cup flour
½ teaspoon baking soda
¼ teaspoon ground cloves
Large pinch of salt
¼ cup dark brown sugar
1 egg
2 tablespoons dark molasses
2 tablespoons corn, cane, birch, or maple syrup
¼ cup fresh ginger, minced
4 tablespoons butter

Grease an 8-inch cake pan or line the bottom with parchment paper. Mix together in a small bowl the flour, baking soda, cloves, salt, and brown sugar.

In a medium bowl, beat together the egg, molasses, syrup, and ginger. Melt the butter gently, then beat it into the molasses mixture. Beat in the flour mixture and pour the batter into the pan.

Bake at 350°F. for 20 to 25 minutes, or until a toothpick as tester comes out clean. Cut into wedges and serve plain or with heavy cream whipped, sour cream, mascarpone, or vanilla ice cream.

Sicilian Biscotti

5 dried figs
⅓ cup raw almonds, skins on
⅓ cup sugar
1 cup flour
¼ cup Dutch cocoa
½ teaspoon ground black pepper
¼ teaspoon baking soda
¼ teaspoon baking powder
¼ teaspoon anise seeds
¼ teaspoon salt
2 eggs, beaten

Discard their stems and chop the figs in a food processor. Add almonds and sugar and process until mixture is finely chopped.

In a small bowl, mix together the flour, cocoa, pepper, baking soda, baking powder, anise, and salt and add to the processor. Pulse until barely mixed. Add the eggs and pulse until well mixed.

Roll the dough into a log about 2 inches in diameter and a foot long. Place the log on a greased baking sheet (or one lined with parchment paper). Bake at 350°F. for 30 minutes.

Remove the pan and lower the oven to 300°F. Cut the log on the diagonal into slices about 1/2-inch thick. Set the slices upright on the baking sheet and return to the oven, letting them bake about 15 minutes more, until they are dry and crisp.

◆ These keep well stored in an airtight tin, but if they lose crispness, you can reheat them at 300°F. for 2 or 3 minutes.

◆ Makes 1½ to 2 dozen.

Orange–Almond Balls

1⅓ cups whole blanched almonds
1½ cups sugar
½ navel orange, rind and all, chopped coarsely
1 tablespoon rum
1 teaspoon almond extract

Put the almonds, 1 cup of the sugar, and the chopped orange into a food processor. Grind the nuts and rind medium fine. Add the rum and almond extract and pulse until mixed.

Sprinkle a cookie sheet with the remaining ½ cup sugar. Pinch off small pieces of the moist dough and roll them into balls about 1 inch in diameter. Roll them in the sugar and arrange them on another sheet to dry for at least 3 hours. Put each in a paper candy cup.

◆ Makes about 3 dozen small balls.

Hazelnut Chocolate Wafers

1 cup toasted hazelnuts, chopped fine
½ cup sugar
6 tablespoons butter, at room temperature
2 egg whites
½ teaspoon vanilla extract
½ cup flour
½ cup high-quality bittersweet chocolate, grated

Grind ½ cup of the nuts with the sugar in a food processor until the nuts are finely ground. Add the butter and pulse until the mixture is smooth. Add the egg whites and vanilla and pulse until well mixed. Add the flour and pulse until barely mixed.

Drop the dough by spoonfuls, about 2 to 3 inches apart, onto a pair of greased cookie sheets (or sheets lined with parchment paper). Flatten the dough with the back of spoon and sprinkle with grated chocolate and chopped nuts.

Bake at 350°F. for 8 to 10 minutes, until edges are browned. Loosen cookies with a spatula while they are warm and let them cool on a rack. Makes about 2 dozen large ones.

Black Chocolate Polenta

½ cup whole-grain polenta
¼ cup cold water
2 cups boiling water
2 ounces bitter chocolate, grated
1 tablespoon ground smoked chili (chipotle, pasilla, mulatto)
2 tablespoons sugar, or to taste
½ teaspoon salt
¼ teaspoon cloves or allspice
2 tablespoons butter
¼ cup toasted almonds
½ teaspoon cinnamon

Put the polenta in the top of a double boiler and moisten it with the cold water. Add the boiling water gradually and stir until smooth. Stir in the grated chocolate, chili, sugar, salt, and cloves. Cover the top and place it over the bottom of the pan, filled with an inch or two of boiling water. Steam until the polenta is thick, then stir in the butter. Pour the polenta into a bowl or platter and sprinkle the top with almonds and cinnamon.

◆ This is particularly good served with crème fraîche.

Index

About the Author

Betty Fussell is a writer who specializes in American food and good home cooking. Her work has appeared in the *New York Times, Vogue, Connoisseur, Journal of Gastronomy, Travel & Leisure,* and other magazines. Her books include *Masters of American Cookery, I Hear America Cooking, Eating In, Food in Good Season, Home Plates, The Story of Corn,* and *Crazy for Corn.* A California native, she now lives in New York City.